The Ultimate Disneyland Paris Travel Companion

Franklin P. Cooper

All rights reserved. No part of this publication may be reproduced, distributed, or transmitted in any form or by any means, including photocopying, recording, or other electronic or mechanical methods, without the prior written permission of the publisher, except in the case of brief quotations embodied in critical reviews and certain other noncommercial uses permitted by copyright law.

Copyright © Franklin P. Cooper, 2025.

About the Author

Franklin Cooper is a seasoned travel writer, researcher, and Disney enthusiast with a passion for crafting **detailed, comprehensive, and engaging travel guides**. With years of experience exploring the world's most iconic destinations, Franklin specializes in **theme parks, cultural landmarks, and immersive travel experiences**.

His deep fascination with **Disney history, theme park design, and guest experience strategies** has led him to meticulously document **every aspect of Disneyland Paris**, ensuring that visitors—whether first-timers or seasoned Disney fans—have all the information they need to plan the perfect trip.

Franklin's travel guides are known for their **authenticity, accuracy, and practicality**, offering not just facts but **insider tips, hidden details, and expert recommendations**. His goal is to help travelers **navigate the magic effortlessly**, saving time, money, and effort while maximizing the fun.

Disneyland Paris remains one of his favorite destinations, and he continues to revisit the park frequently to ensure his guides stay **up-to-date and relevant**.

Table of Contents

Introduction……………………………………………..………..8

Overview of Disneyland Paris……………………………………..…..8

Why Visit?..12

History and Development……………………………………………19

Chapter 1

Planning Your Trip…………………………………………...28

Best Time to Visit……………………………………..………..28

How Many Days to Stay……………………………………….34

Budgeting and Cost Breakdown…………………………….41

Chapter 2

Getting There……………………………………………….51

Transportation Options (Flights, Trains, Buses, Driving)…………51

From Paris to Disneyland Paris……………………………………...64

Chapter 3

Tickets & Packages……………………………………….....71

Ticket Types and Prices………………………………………...71

Annual Passes……………………………………………….77

Special Offers and Discounts………………………………..79

4

Chapter 4

Accommodation...**84**

Official Disneyland Hotels...84

Nearby Partner Hotels..89

Budget vs. Luxury Options...91

Chapter 5

Parks Overview...**95**

Disneyland Park..95

Walt Disney Studios Park...98

Chapter 6

Disneyland Park..**103**

Main Street, U.S.A...103

Frontierland..109

Adventureland..116

Fantasyland...120

Discoveryland...123

Chapter 7

Walt Disney Studios Park..**131**

Studio 1 & Production Courtyard...131

Avengers Campus..134

Toy Story Playland...137

Ratatouille and Paris-themed Attractions.............................140

Upcoming Attractions..142

Chapter 8

Rides & Attractions...143

Must-Do Rides...143

Family-Friendly Attractions...146

Thrill Rides..149

Shows and Parades..153

Chapter 9

Dining & Food..156

Best Restaurants in the Parks...156

Character Dining Experiences...159

Budget-Friendly Eats...161

Chapter 10

Shopping & Merchandise..168

Best Shops for Souvenirs...168

Exclusive Merchandise..172

Collectibles & Limited-Edition Items..............................174

Chapter 11

Entertainment & Special Events…………………..……...180

Seasonal Events (Halloween, Christmas, etc.)……………...…180

Fireworks & Nighttime Shows…………………………………182

Character Meet & Greets…………....……………………….183

Chapter 12

Tips & Tricks for a Smooth Visit………………………....…186

Best Ways to Avoid Long Queues....................................186

Mobile Apps and Tech Tips…………………………………....…192

Accessibility and Disability Services………………....……….194

Conclusion

Final Thoughts & Recommendations……………………....…199

Introduction

Overview of Disneyland Paris

A World of Magic in Europe

Disneyland Paris is **Europe's most visited theme park resort**, attracting millions of visitors every year. Located in **Marne-la-Vallée**, about **32 kilometers (20 miles) east of Paris**, the resort is a vast entertainment complex that blends **Disney's storytelling magic with French culture**, offering a unique experience for visitors of all ages.

Originally opened as **Euro Disney Resort on April 12, 1992**, the park went through financial challenges and public criticism before evolving into a beloved destination. It was renamed **Disneyland Paris in 1995** and has since become one of the most successful Disney parks outside the United States.

The resort spans approximately **2,230 hectares (5,500 acres)**, making it one of the largest Disney properties globally. It consists of:

Disneyland Park – The heart of the resort, inspired by Walt Disney's original Disneyland in California. This park features classic fairytale settings, immersive lands, thrilling attractions, and spectacular shows.

Walt Disney Studios Park – Opened in 2002, this park celebrates filmmaking, animation, and the magic behind Disney movies, with attractions based on **Pixar, Marvel, and Hollywood cinema**.

Disney Village – A lively **shopping, dining, and entertainment district** located just outside the parks, accessible to both visitors and non-park guests.

Seven Official Disney Hotels – Each uniquely themed, offering immersive accommodations ranging from budget-friendly to luxury experiences.

Partner Hotels – A collection of hotels near the resort that provide alternative lodging options with convenient access to Disneyland Paris.

A European Disney Experience

Disneyland Paris combines **Disney's iconic themes with European culture**, making it different from its American counterparts. While it retains many classic Disney attractions, it also features unique elements inspired by **French art, history, and storytelling traditions**.

One of the park's standout features is **Sleeping Beauty Castle (Le Château de la Belle au Bois Dormant)**, which is considered by many to be the most beautiful Disney castle ever built. Unlike other Disney castles, this one was **designed with a fairy-tale European aesthetic**, incorporating medieval French influences, stained-glass windows, and a mysterious dragon animatronic hidden in its dungeons—an exclusive feature only found in Disneyland Paris.

The resort is also home to **some of the most advanced Disney attractions in the world**, such as:

Ratatouille: The Adventure – A 4D dark ride that shrinks visitors down to the size of a rat, immersing them in a Parisian kitchen.

Avengers Assemble: Flight Force – A high-speed roller coaster featuring Iron Man and Captain Marvel, exclusive to Disneyland Paris.

Phantom Manor – A reimagined version of the Haunted Mansion, featuring a darker Western ghost story with a mysterious backstory unique to Disneyland Paris.

Growth and Popularity

Since its opening, **over 320 million visitors** have passed through the gates of Disneyland Paris, solidifying its status as one of the **top tourist destinations in Europe**. The resort has undergone major expansions, including the addition of **new themed areas, attractions, and hotels**. The latest expansions, including a **Marvel-**

themed **Avengers Campus** and the upcoming **Frozen and Star Wars lands**, aim to make Disneyland Paris even more immersive and competitive with other international Disney parks.

More Than Just a Theme Park

While Disneyland Paris is famous for its **thrilling rides and magical atmosphere**, it also offers:

World-class dining experiences, from **Michelin-starred restaurants** to classic Disney snacks with a French twist (such as Mickey-shaped macarons).

Unforgettable entertainment, including parades, fireworks, and stage shows exclusive to Disneyland Paris.

Seasonal events, such as **Disney Halloween Festival, Disney Enchanted Christmas**, and **Disneyland Paris Pride**, offering unique experiences throughout the year.

A Destination for All Travelers

Whether you're a **first-time visitor, a Disney enthusiast, a family with kids, or a solo traveler**, Disneyland Paris has something to offer. The resort provides various accessibility options, family-friendly services, and multi-day ticket packages to suit different travel needs.

From **storybook castles to cinematic adventures**, Disneyland Paris is a **dream destination** where European charm meets

Why Visit Disneyland Paris?

Disneyland Paris is more than just a theme park—it's a **magical experience** that brings Disney's world-renowned storytelling to life in a **distinctly European setting**. Whether you're a **first-time visitor or a lifelong Disney fan**, this resort offers a **unique combination of thrilling rides, enchanting atmospheres, world-class dining, and unforgettable entertainment**.

If you're wondering **why Disneyland Paris deserves a place on your travel itinerary**, here are the most compelling reasons:

1. A Unique Disney Park with European Elegance

Unlike its counterparts in the **United States, Japan, or China**, Disneyland Paris incorporates **French culture and European artistry** into its design, making it a one-of-a-kind destination.

The park's architecture and décor are inspired by **French fairy tales, medieval castles, and European art history**.

Attractions like **Le Château de la Belle au Bois Dormant (Sleeping Beauty Castle)** feature **stained-glass windows and hand-painted tapestries**, showcasing exquisite craftsmanship.

The landscaping is **meticulously designed**, with gardens that **change seasonally** to reflect different themes throughout the year.

Even the **background music** throughout the park includes **orchestrated Disney scores with a classical European influence**, adding to the elegant atmosphere.

2. The Most Beautiful Disney Castle in the World

Disneyland Paris is home to **what many consider to be the most breathtaking Disney castle ever built—Le Château de la Belle au Bois Dormant (Sleeping Beauty Castle).**

Unlike the traditional towering structures in other parks, this **pink and blue masterpiece** was designed to complement **Europe's rich history of real-life castles** while maintaining a whimsical fairy-tale look.

The castle features:

Golden turrets and stained-glass windows inspired by real medieval European cathedrals.

A **mystical underground dungeon** where guests can see **La Tanière du Dragon (The Dragon's Lair)**—a **massive animatronic dragon**, unique to Disneyland Paris.

Hidden details and Easter eggs referencing the **classic Sleeping Beauty film and European folklore.**

Whether you admire it from afar or explore its **mystical interiors**, the Disneyland Paris castle is a **must-see landmark** that sets this resort apart from all other Disney parks.

3. Exclusive Attractions You Won't Find Anywhere Else

While Disneyland Paris features many classic Disney rides, it also boasts **exclusive attractions that can't be found in any other Disney park.**

Disneyland Park Unique Attractions:

Phantom Manor – A darker, spookier version of **Haunted Mansion**, with a complex **Wild West ghost story**.

Indiana Jones and the Temple of Peril – A high-speed roller coaster that **features an inversion**, unlike any other Disney Indiana Jones ride.

Alice's Curious Labyrinth – A **walk-through maze** inspired by *Alice in Wonderland*, where guests can explore and climb the Queen of Hearts' castle.

Walt Disney Studios Park Unique Attractions:

Ratatouille: The Adventure – A **4D trackless ride** where guests are **shrunk to the size of a rat** and scurry through a Parisian kitchen.

Avengers Assemble: Flight Force – A **fast-paced Marvel roller coaster** featuring Iron Man and Captain Marvel, exclusive to Disneyland Paris.

Cars ROAD TRIP – A scenic drive through the world of *Cars*, featuring impressive **animatronics and special effects**.

These **exclusive rides** make Disneyland Paris a **must-visit destination for Disney fans** who want to experience something new.

4. Spectacular Entertainment & Live Shows

Disneyland Paris offers some of the **best Disney parades, stage shows, and nighttime spectaculars** in the world.

Disney Stars on Parade – A **lavish daily parade** featuring beautifully designed floats, beloved Disney characters, and **stunning choreography**.

Disney Illuminations – A **fireworks and projection show** over Sleeping Beauty Castle, incorporating **scenes from Disney, Pixar, and Star Wars films**.

Mickey and the Magician – An award-winning **stage show blending illusions, music, and live performances**, exclusive to Disneyland Paris.

The resort also hosts **special seasonal events**, such as:

Disney Halloween Festival – Featuring **villain takeovers, eerie decorations, and exclusive nighttime entertainment**.

Disney Enchanted Christmas – A **winter wonderland transformation** with **snowfall on Main Street, a magical Christmas parade, and festive treats**.

Disneyland Paris Pride – A celebration of **diversity and inclusion**, featuring concerts, meet-and-greets, and a vibrant **pride parade**.

If you love **immersive shows, dazzling fireworks, and lively entertainment**, Disneyland Paris offers some of the **best performances in any Disney park**.

5. A Foodie's Paradise – French-Inspired Disney Dining

Unlike other theme parks, Disneyland Paris is **renowned for its refined culinary experiences**, blending **Disney magic with world-class French cuisine**.

Must-Try Dining Experiences:

Bistrot Chez Rémy – A **Ratatouille-themed French bistro** where guests dine at **rat-sized tables**, enjoying gourmet dishes like **steak frites and ratatouille**.

Auberge de Cendrillon – A **royal dining experience** featuring **classic French meals** and **meet-and-greets with Disney princesses**.

Walt's – An American Restaurant – A **fine-dining tribute to Walt Disney**, serving **classic American and European fusion cuisine**.

Even quick-service restaurants feature **French specialties** like **crêpes, éclairs, and freshly baked baguettes**, making Disneyland Paris **one of the best Disney parks for food lovers**.

6. Easy Access from Paris & Across Europe

Disneyland Paris is one of the **most accessible Disney resorts in the world**, making it an easy **day trip or weekend getaway** from Paris and other European cities.

From Central Paris: The **RER A train** takes just **35 minutes** from Paris to **Marne-la-Vallée – Chessy station**, located right at the park entrance.

From London & Brussels: The **Eurostar train** offers a **direct route to Disneyland Paris**, making it **a convenient option for international travelers**.

From Charles de Gaulle Airport: Direct shuttles and high-speed trains take visitors **from the airport to the park in less than 15 minutes.**

Whether you're traveling from within France or internationally, Disneyland Paris is **one of the most convenient Disney parks to visit.**

7. A Perfect Destination for Families, Couples & Disney Fans

Disneyland Paris offers something for **every type of traveler**:

For Families: The park is **designed for all ages**, with **kid-friendly attractions, playgrounds, and character meet-and-greets.**

For Couples: Disneyland Paris is a **romantic getaway**, featuring **candlelit dining, stunning castle views, and fairytale-themed experiences.**

For Disney Fans: The resort is packed with **hidden details, unique merchandise, and classic Disney magic** that make it a **must-visit for any Disney enthusiast.**

With **ongoing expansions**, including upcoming **Frozen, Star Wars, and Marvel lands**, Disneyland Paris is **constantly evolving**, offering new experiences with every visit.

Why Disneyland Paris is a Must-Visit Destination

Disneyland Paris is more than just a theme park—it's an **unforgettable Disney experience infused with European charm**. Whether you're seeking **thrilling rides, immersive shows, world-class dining, or simply the magic of Disney**, this resort delivers on every level.

With its **breathtaking castle, exclusive attractions, spectacular entertainment, and easy access from Paris**, Disneyland Paris is a **must-visit destination** for travelers from around the world.

History and Development of Disneyland Paris

Disneyland Paris, the **first and only Disney resort in Europe**, has a fascinating history marked by **ambitious vision, controversy, cultural adaptation, and ultimate success**. From its conception in the **1980s** to its present-day status as one of the **most visited theme parks in Europe**, the journey of Disneyland Paris is a tale of **challenges, growth, and enduring Disney magic**.

1. The Origins: How Disneyland Came to Europe

Following the success of **Disneyland (California, 1955) and Walt Disney World (Florida, 1971)**, The Walt Disney Company began looking for **an ideal European location** to expand its theme park empire.

The Search for the Perfect Location (1970s – Early 1980s)

Disney executives analyzed **over 1,200 locations** across **Germany, Spain, Italy, the United Kingdom, and France**.

Spain was a strong contender due to its **sunny weather**, but France's central location in Europe and strong tourism industry made it a more strategic choice.

Ultimately, in **1985**, Disney chose **Marne-la-Vallée, France**, a rural area **32 km (20 miles) east of Paris**, due to:

Its proximity to **Paris, one of the most visited cities in the world**.

Strong **transportation networks** (including plans for a high-speed rail connection).

Generous **financial incentives and tax breaks** from the French government.

The Controversial Agreement with France

The French government played a major role in the project, offering **infrastructure investments and tax incentives** to secure the deal.

In exchange, Disney agreed to:

Create **thousands of jobs** for French citizens.

Preserve **French cultural identity** in the park's design, food, and atmosphere.

Build a **high-end tourism complex**, including hotels, golf courses, and future expansions.

With an agreement in place, construction on **"Euro Disneyland"** (its original name) officially began in **1988**.

2. The Grand Opening and Early Struggles (1992 – Mid 1990s)

Opening Day: April 12, 1992

After four years of construction, **Euro Disneyland opened to the public on April 12, 1992**. The resort included:

Disneyland Park (the main theme park).

Seven Disney-themed hotels.

A shopping and entertainment complex (now known as Disney Village).

Golf Disneyland, an 18-hole golf course.

Cultural Clashes and Initial Struggles

Despite high expectations, the early years of Euro Disneyland were challenging due to:

1. French Resistance to Americanization

Many critics feared that Disney's presence would lead to the **"cultural invasion" of American consumerism** in France.

French intellectuals and journalists criticized the project, with one famously calling it **"a cultural Chernobyl."**

Some employees went on strike due to the **strict Disney grooming and behavior policies**, which clashed with French workplace norms.

2. Lower-Than-Expected Attendance

Disney **overestimated European demand**, expecting **11 million visitors in the first year** but only reaching **9 million**.

The recession in Europe at the time **reduced disposable income**, leading to lower ticket sales.

Many Europeans found ticket prices and hotel costs **too expensive**.

3. Financial Crisis & Near Bankruptcy (1994)

By **1994**, Disneyland Paris was facing **severe financial problems**, with **$3 billion in debt**. The resort was on the verge of **bankruptcy**, leading to:

A **financial restructuring** plan led by Disney and banks.

More affordable hotel options to **attract middle-class families**.

The introduction of **alcohol sales** in restaurants to better align with French dining culture.

3. The Turning Point: Rebranding & Revival (1995 – 2000s)

1995: The Success of Space Mountain & Rebranding

The park's major turnaround began with the launch of **Space Mountain: De la Terre à la Lune** in **1995**. This ride, based on **Jules Verne's classic novel**, became an instant success due to:

A **uniquely European theme** appealing to local audiences.

Thrilling elements, including a **high-speed launch and inversions** (unlike its U.S. versions).

A **massive marketing campaign** that helped boost attendance.

Following this success, in **1995**, Disney **renamed the park from "Euro Disneyland" to "Disneyland Paris"**, giving it a **more local identity**.

By the late 1990s, the park was **profitable for the first time**, attracting **over 12 million visitors annually**.

4. Expansion & Growth: The Birth of Walt Disney Studios Park (2002 – 2010s)

2002: Walt Disney Studios Park Opens

To further establish Disneyland Paris as a **multi-day destination**, a **second theme park**, **Walt Disney Studios Park**, opened in **2002**.

Dedicated to **the magic of filmmaking, animation, and special effects**.

Featured attractions like **CinéMagique, Studio Tram Tour, and Moteurs... Action! Stunt Show Spectacular**.

Initially **struggled** due to a lack of major attractions but gradually expanded.

The 2000s: Continued Growth and Upgrades

Disneyland Paris saw **significant developments**:

The Twilight Zone Tower of Terror (2007) – A Hollywood-themed **drop tower attraction**, improving Walt Disney Studios Park.

Toy Story Playland (2010) – A **family-friendly expansion** with rides based on *Toy Story*.

A major refurbishment program to improve older attractions.

By 2012, Disneyland Paris celebrated its **20th anniversary**, attracting over **16 million annual visitors**.

5. Disneyland Paris Today: New Era & Expansion (2018 – Present)

Disney Buys Full Ownership (2017)

For years, Disneyland Paris operated as a **joint venture**, with Disney only holding **a minority stake**. In 2017, The Walt Disney Company **bought full ownership** of Disneyland Paris, allowing for:

More direct control over park management and expansion.

Major financial investments for long-term development.

Massive €2 Billion Expansion (Announced in 2018)

Disney announced a **€2 billion expansion project**, bringing **three massive new lands** to **Walt Disney Studios Park**:

1. **Avengers Campus** (opened in 2022) – A Marvel-themed land with attractions like **Avengers Assemble: Flight Force** and **Spider-Man W.E.B. Adventure**.

2. **Frozen Land (Opening 2025)** – A fully immersive *Frozen* area, featuring Arendelle Castle, a boat ride, and themed shops/restaurants.

3. **Star Wars Land (Future Plans)** – Expected to bring a **galaxy far, far away** to Disneyland Paris.

Post-COVID Recovery & Future Growth

Despite the **temporary closure during the COVID-19 pandemic**, Disneyland Paris has bounced back stronger than ever, with:

A complete refurbishment of classic attractions.

New nighttime shows, entertainment, and special events.

Increased investment in sustainability and guest experience.

Disneyland Paris – From Struggle to Success

From its **controversial beginnings** to its status as **Europe's top tourist destination**, Disneyland Paris has proven to be a **remarkable success story**.

Despite **initial financial struggles, cultural adaptation challenges, and economic downturns**, the park **reinvented itself** with:

Immersive expansions (Walt Disney Studios Park, Avengers Campus, Frozen Land).

A deep connection to European storytelling (Space Mountain, Ratatouille).

A commitment to quality, magic, and guest experience.

With **millions of visitors annually**, Disneyland Paris continues to **grow, evolve, and bring Disney magic to generations of guests**.

Chapter 1

Planning Your Trip

Best Time to Visit Disneyland Paris

Choosing the best time to visit Disneyland Paris is crucial for ensuring a **memorable experience** with **shorter wait times, better weather, and more entertainment options**. The best time depends on **your priorities**—whether you prefer **low crowds, budget-friendly options, seasonal events, or ideal weather**.

1. Crowd Levels & Peak vs. Off-Peak Seasons

Disneyland Paris experiences **varying crowd levels** throughout the year. Understanding peak and off-peak seasons will help you choose a time that best suits your preferences.

Peak Season (High Crowds & Longer Wait Times)

These periods bring the **largest crowds, longest queues, and highest prices**, but also feature **extended hours, parades, and special events**.

Peak periods include:

Summer Holidays (July – August)

Extremely **high crowd levels** as families across Europe visit during school vacations.

Hot weather (25°C–35°C / 77°F–95°F) but manageable with indoor attractions.

Longer park hours (open until 11 PM) with **nighttime shows**.

Expensive hotel rates & flights due to summer tourism.

Christmas & New Year (Mid-November – Early January)
The park transforms into a **winter wonderland** with **festive decorations, snowfall effects, and Christmas-themed parades**.

Special events like **Mickey's Christmas Big Band, Disney Enchanted Christmas, and New Year's Eve fireworks**.

Cold weather (0°C–10°C / 32°F–50°F) but magical holiday vibes.

Extremely crowded, especially from **December 20 – January 6**.

Easter & Spring Break (March – April)
Moderate to high crowds due to school holidays across Europe.

Pleasant **spring weather (10°C–20°C / 50°F–68°F)** with blooming flowers.

Special **Easter decorations and character meet-and-greets**.

Prices **increase significantly**, especially around Easter weekend.

Off-Peak Season (Lower Crowds & Budget-Friendly)
For visitors who prefer **shorter lines, quieter parks, and lower prices**, off-peak periods are the best choice.

Best off-peak months:
Mid-January – Mid-March (After Christmas rush, before Easter holidays).

Mid-September – Early October (After summer holidays, before Halloween season).

Why visit in the off-season?

Lower hotel and ticket prices (except during promotional events).
Shorter wait times (most rides have a **5-20 minute queue** instead of 60+ minutes).
Cooler weather, making it easier to walk around.
Fewer shows and entertainment (some parades and nighttime shows may be canceled).
Shorter park hours (closing as early as 6-7 PM). Some **rides might be closed for maintenance**.

2. Weather Considerations: Best Seasons to Visit

Disneyland Paris is a **year-round destination**, but the **seasonal weather** can affect your experience.

Season	Pros	Cons
Spring (March – May)	Mild temperatures (10°C–20°C) Flowers in bloom Easter events	Rain showers possible Some school holidays mean moderate crowds
Summer (June – August)	Long park hours Nighttime shows All attractions open	Very crowded High prices Can be hot (up to 35°C)
Autumn (September – November)	Fewer crowds (Sept & early Oct) Halloween festival Mild temperatures (10°C–18°C)	Rain increases in Nov Some attractions under refurbishment
Winter (December – February)	Magical Christmas decorations Festive events Fewer crowds in Jan-Feb	Very cold (0°C–7°C) Some outdoor rides may close Shorter daylight hours

3. Best Time for Budget Travelers

If you're looking for **cheaper tickets, hotel deals, and affordable flights**, consider:

Mid-January to Mid-March (Post-holiday discounts).

Mid-September to Early October (Fewer tourists, lower prices).

Weekdays (Tuesday – Thursday) are **cheaper than weekends**.

Pro Tip: Check for Disneyland Paris **seasonal discounts and special promotions** on their official website.

4. Best Time for Families with Kids

If you're traveling with children, consider:

May or September (mild weather, fewer crowds).

Midweek (Tuesday – Thursday) to avoid weekend rush.

Christmas (December) or Halloween (October) for magical seasonal experiences.

Avoid: Summer (July-August) unless you're prepared for long waits and heat.

5. Best Time for Special Events & Seasonal Celebrations

If you love **special Disney experiences**, time your visit during one of these festivals:

Halloween Festival (October – Early November)

Disney Halloween Festival – Spooky decorations, villain meet-and-greets, and special parades. **Disney Halloween Party (October 31st)** – A separate ticket event with **exclusive shows & late-night access**.

Christmas & New Year's Celebrations (Mid-November – Early January)

Disney Enchanted Christmas – Stunning holiday lights, snowfall on Main Street, and a Christmas parade. **New Year's Eve Party (December 31st)** – Fireworks, concerts, and extended hours.

RunDisney (April or September)

Marathon event where guests can run through the park and meet Disney characters.

Disneyland Paris Pride (June)

A special after-hours event celebrating LGBTQ+ pride with concerts and exclusive shows.

How Many Days to Stay at Disneyland Paris?

Deciding how many days to spend at **Disneyland Paris** depends on several factors, including **what you want to experience, crowd levels, personal preferences, and travel constraints**. While some visitors attempt to explore the parks in **one day**, a well-planned trip typically requires **at least two to three days** to fully enjoy everything Disneyland Paris has to offer.

1. Key Factors to Consider

A. Number of Parks

Disneyland Paris is a **two-park resort**:

1. **Disneyland Park** – The classic Disney experience with **five themed lands, iconic attractions, and shows**.

2. **Walt Disney Studios Park** – A movie-themed park with **thrill rides, immersive lands (like Avengers Campus), and behind-the-scenes entertainment**.

If you want to **properly experience both parks**, at least **two full days** are recommended.

B. Attractions and Experiences

Disneyland Paris offers **over 50 rides**, plus parades, shows, character meet-and-greets, and themed restaurants. Some major attractions include:

Disneyland Park: Big Thunder Mountain, Pirates of the Caribbean, Phantom Manor, It's a Small World, Sleeping Beauty Castle, and Space Mountain.

Walt Disney Studios Park: Avengers Assemble: Flight Force, Spider-Man W.E.B. Adventure, The Twilight Zone Tower of Terror, and Ratatouille: The Adventure.

If you want to experience **every major ride and show**, you'll need at least **two to three days** to avoid rushing.

C. Crowd Levels and Wait Times

Crowds **greatly affect** how much you can do in a day.

Peak Seasons (Summer, Christmas, Easter, Halloween) – Long wait times (60+ minutes for top rides) may limit how much you can experience in one day.

Low Seasons (Mid-January to March, Mid-September to Mid-October) – Shorter queues allow you to experience more in less time.

During busy times, **a one-day visit may feel rushed**, whereas a **multi-day visit** allows for a more relaxed experience.

D. Special Events and Seasonal Celebrations

Disneyland Paris frequently hosts **special events** that may influence your stay duration:

Disney Halloween Festival (September – October)

Disney Enchanted Christmas (November – Early January)

RunDisney Races

Electroland (Summer Music Festival)

If you want to enjoy these seasonal events **without sacrificing rides and attractions**, staying at least **three days** is ideal.

E. Travel Fatigue and Park Hopping

Disneyland Paris involves a **lot of walking**, with an average of **10-15 km (6-9 miles) per day**. If you rush through everything in one day, you may feel exhausted and unable to fully enjoy the experience. **A two- or three-day visit** allows for a more relaxed pace.

2. Suggested Stay Durations

A. One Day (Only if You're Short on Time)

A **one-day trip** is possible, but only recommended if:

You **only want to visit one park** (either Disneyland Park or Walt Disney Studios Park).

You're fine with **missing some attractions** due to time constraints.

You use **Premier Access** (paid fast passes) to skip long queues.

If doing **both parks in one day**, focus on:

Disneyland Park: Sleeping Beauty Castle, Big Thunder Mountain, Pirates of the Caribbean, and Phantom Manor.

Walt Disney Studios Park: Avengers Campus, Ratatouille, and The Twilight Zone Tower of Terror.

Downsides: A **one-day visit can feel rushed**, with limited time for parades, shows, or dining.

B. Two Days (Recommended for First-Time Visitors)

A **two-day visit** is ideal for those who want a balanced experience:

Day 1: Disneyland Park (explore lands, watch parades, enjoy classic attractions).

Day 2: Walt Disney Studios Park (experience Marvel rides, Ratatouille, and thrill rides).

Pros:
Enough time for all the major attractions.

Can enjoy shows and meet characters. Less stress compared to a one-day trip.

Downsides: May still feel rushed during peak seasons.

C. Three Days (Ideal for a Full Experience)

A **three-day visit** is the perfect way to experience everything:

Day 1: Focus on Disneyland Park's main attractions.

Day 2: Focus on Walt Disney Studios Park, including Avengers Campus.

Day 3: Revisit favorites, explore hidden details, and enjoy parades and shows.

Pros:
Allows for a relaxed pace and better immersion. Ideal for families with young children. Time for shopping, fine dining, and seasonal events.

Downsides: More expensive due to additional hotel nights.

D. Four to Five Days (For Ultimate Disney Fans & Families)

A **four- or five-day** trip is best if you want to:

Explore every attraction at a **slow and immersive pace**.

Repeat favorite rides **multiple times**.

Experience **every show, parade, and nighttime spectacular**.

Visit **Disney Village**, try **various restaurants**, and shop for souvenirs.

Pros:
No rushing—enjoy every detail at leisure. Perfect for families with young kids needing breaks. Full experience of seasonal events and character interactions.

Downsides: Higher cost, but **worth it for true Disney lovers**.

3. Cost Considerations for Multi-Day Trips

The longer you stay, the more budget planning is needed:

Park Tickets: Multi-day tickets are cheaper per day than single-day tickets.

Hotels: Staying at **Disney hotels** offers benefits like **Early Magic Hours**, but staying offsite can save money.

Food & Dining: More days mean **higher meal costs**—consider **meal plans or bringing snacks**.

4. Best Length Based on Traveler Type

Traveler Type	Recommended Stay	Reason
Solo Travelers	1-2 Days	Can move quickly and prioritize top attractions.
Families with Kids	3-4 Days	Allows for breaks, character meets, and a relaxed pace.
First-Time Visitors	2-3 Days	Enough time to experience both parks without rushing.
Disney Enthusiasts	4-5 Days	Full immersion, repeat rides, and enjoy all experiences.
Budget Travelers	1-2 Days	Limits accommodation and food costs while still enjoying the parks.

Budgeting and Cost Breakdown for Disneyland Paris

A trip to **Disneyland Paris** can be a **magical** experience, but proper budgeting is crucial to avoid unexpected expenses. Costs can vary depending on the season, accommodation, ticket types, and personal preferences. Below is a **detailed breakdown** of all major expenses, along with **money-saving tips** to help plan a cost-effective trip.

1. Key Factors That Affect Your Budget

Before diving into costs, here are the main factors that determine your Disneyland Paris budget:

1. **Time of Visit**

Peak Season (High Prices): Summer (June–August), Christmas, Easter, Halloween.

Off-Peak Season (Lower Prices): January–March, mid-September–early December.

2. **Accommodation Choice**

On-site Disney hotels are the most convenient but expensive.

Partner and off-site hotels offer more budget-friendly alternatives.

3. **Type of Park Ticket**

Single-day vs. Multi-day tickets: The more days you stay, the lower the cost per day.

Standard vs. Premier Access: Premier Access costs more but helps skip long lines.

4. **Dining Preferences**

Quick-service vs. Table-service dining: Buffets and table-service restaurants cost significantly more.

Bringing snacks can help cut down food costs.

5. **Transportation to Disneyland Paris**

Flying vs. Train vs. Driving: Costs vary based on your location and travel method.

6. **Additional Expenses**

Souvenirs, Genie+ services, special experiences (e.g., character dining).

2. Cost Breakdown by Category

A. Park Tickets

Ticket Type	Adults (12+)	Children (3-11)	Notes
1-Day 1-Park Ticket	€62 – €105	€57 – €97	Price varies by season
1-Day 2-Park Ticket	€87 – €130	€82 – €122	Allows entry to both parks
2-Day Ticket (Both Parks)	€139 – €210	€129 – €195	Multi-day tickets offer better value
3-Day Ticket (Both Parks)	€176 – €269	€164 – €249	
4-Day Ticket (Both Parks)	€209 – €322	€194 – €299	
Annual Passes	€289 – €719	Same as adult pricing	Different tiers offer various perks
Premier Access (Skip	€90 – €190 per	N/A	Available for select rides

Ticket Type	Adults (12+)	Children (3-11)	Notes
Lines)		ride	

Money-Saving Tips:

Book tickets in advance for lower prices.

Visit during off-peak seasons to get cheaper rates.

Consider **multi-day tickets** for better value per day.

B. Accommodation Costs

Hotel Category	Hotel Example	Price Per Night (Approx.)
Luxury Disney Hotels	Disneyland Hotel (5★)	€700 – €2,000
Deluxe Disney Hotels	Disney's Hotel New York – The Art of Marvel (4★)	€400 – €700
Moderate Disney Hotels	Disney's Newport Bay Club (4★)	€250 – €500

Hotel Category	Hotel Example	Price Per Night (Approx.)
Value Disney Hotels	Disney's Santa Fe / Cheyenne (3 ★)	€150 – €350
Disney Partner Hotels	Explorers Hotel, Campanile Val de France	€80 – €200
Budget Off-Site Hotels	Ibis Marne-la-Vallée, B&B Hotel	€60 – €150
Airbnb/Rental Apartments	Varies	€50 – €200

Money-Saving Tips:

Stay at **Disney's budget hotels** (*Santa Fe, Cheyenne*) for a cheaper on-site experience.

Consider **partner hotels** with free shuttles to Disneyland.

Use **Airbnb or nearby hotels** for budget-friendly alternatives.

C. Transportation Costs
1. Getting to Disneyland Paris

Transport Mode	Estimated Cost (Round Trip)	Details
Flight (International)	€100 – €800	Varies by country & airline
Train (Eurostar from London)	€50 – €250	Direct train from London to Disneyland
TGV Train from Paris	€20 – €40	10-minute ride from Paris Gare de Lyon
Bus from Paris	€15 – €25	Budget-friendly but slower
Taxi from Paris	€70 – €100	Convenient but expensive
Rental Car	€50 – €100 per day	Parking at Disneyland: €30 per day

2. Getting Around Disneyland Paris

Walking: The two parks and hotels are within **walking distance**.

Free shuttle buses: Available between Disney hotels and the parks.

Money-Saving Tips:
Use **TGV or RER A train** instead of taxis.

Avoid car rentals unless necessary (parking fees are high).

D. Food & Dining Costs

Dining Option	Average Price per Meal	Examples
Quick-Service (Fast Food)	€12 – €20	Casey's Corner, Pizzeria Bella Notte
Buffet Restaurants	€35 – €50	Plaza Gardens, Agrabah Café
Table-Service Restaurants	€40 – €70	Captain Jack's, Bistrot Chez Rémy
Character Dining	€60 – €120	Auberge de Cendrillon, Plaza

Dining Option	Average Price per Meal	Examples
		Gardens
Snacks & Drinks	€5 – €15	Popcorn, Mickey-shaped treats
Self-Catering	€5 – €10	Grocery store meals, packed food

Money-Saving Tips:

Bring **snacks and bottled water**.

Eat at **Disney Village or nearby hotels** for cheaper options.

Opt for **quick-service meals** instead of table service.

E. Souvenirs & Extras

Item	Estimated Cost
Mickey Ears	€20 – €30
Plush Toys	€25 – €50
Spirit Jerseys	€60 – €80
Pins & Collectibles	€10 – €25 each

Item	Estimated Cost
Ride Photos	€15 – €20
Light-up Toys	€20 – €40

Money-Saving Tips:

Buy Disney merchandise **before your trip** (cheaper online).

Set a **souvenir budget** to avoid overspending.

F. Total Estimated Budget

Category	Budget Option (€)	Mid-Range (€)	Luxury (€)
Park Tickets	62 – 139	140 – 269	270 – 719
Accommodation (2 nights)	100 – 300	400 – 800	1000 – 3000
Transportation	20 – 100	100 – 300	300 – 800
Food & Drinks	50 – 100	120 – 200	300 – 600
Souvenirs & Extras	30 – 80	100 – 200	300+
Total (Per Person)	**€262 – €719**	**€860 – €1,769**	**€2,170 – €6,119**

Final Tips to Save Money at Disneyland Paris

Book in advance for better deals on tickets and hotels.
Visit during the off-season for lower prices.
Stay off-site for budget-friendly accommodations.
Use meal deals and share portions to save on food.
Use free transport options (shuttles, walking).

By carefully planning and budgeting, you can enjoy the **magic of Disneyland Paris** without overspending!

Chapter 2

Getting There

Transportation Options (Flights, Trains, Buses, Driving)

Flights

Disneyland Paris is one of the most accessible theme parks in Europe, with multiple transportation options available for travelers from different parts of the world. Flying is the fastest and most convenient way to reach Disneyland Paris, especially for international visitors. Below is a **detailed guide** on flight options, major airports, and essential contact information.

1. Airports Near Disneyland Paris

The closest airport to Disneyland Paris is **Paris Charles de Gaulle Airport (CDG)**, but travelers can also fly into **Orly Airport (ORY)** or **Beauvais-Tillé Airport (BVA)** depending on their departure location and budget.

A. Charles de Gaulle Airport (CDG) – Best Option

Distance to Disneyland Paris: ~35 km (22 miles)

Travel Time: 10–45 minutes (depending on transportation choice)

Why Choose CDG?:

Largest and busiest airport in France

Well-connected with direct train and shuttle services to Disneyland

Serves major international and domestic flights

Contact Information:

Website: www.parisaeroport.fr

Phone: +33 1 70 36 39 50

B. Orly Airport (ORY) – Secondary Option
Distance to Disneyland Paris: ~45 km (28 miles)

Travel Time: 45–60 minutes

Why Choose ORY?:
Smaller and less crowded than CDG

Ideal for flights within Europe

Shuttle and train options available, though slightly less direct

Contact Information:

Website: www.parisaeroport.fr

Phone: +33 892 56 39 50

C. Beauvais-Tillé Airport (BVA) – Budget Option
Distance to Disneyland Paris: ~120 km (75 miles)

Travel Time: 1.5–2 hours

Why Choose BVA?:
Best for budget travelers using low-cost airlines (Ryanair, Wizz Air)

Cheaper flights but longer travel time to Disneyland

Contact Information:

Website: www.aeroportparisbeauvais.com

Phone: +33 3 44 11 46 66

2. Airlines Flying to Paris

Numerous airlines offer direct and connecting flights to **Paris Charles de Gaulle (CDG) and Orly (ORY)** from all over the world. Here are some major airlines flying into Paris:

North America to Paris

Air France (www.airfrance.com) – Direct flights from New York (JFK), Los Angeles (LAX), Miami (MIA), Chicago (ORD), and more.

Delta Airlines (www.delta.com) – Operates direct flights from Atlanta, Boston, and New York.

United Airlines (www.united.com) – Flights from Newark, Washington D.C., and Chicago.

American Airlines (www.aa.com) – Services from Dallas, Philadelphia, and Charlotte.

Air Canada (www.aircanada.com) – Direct flights from Toronto, Montreal, and Vancouver.

Europe to Paris

British Airways (www.britishairways.com) – Flights from London, Manchester, and Edinburgh.

Lufthansa (www.lufthansa.com) – Flights from Frankfurt, Munich, and Berlin.

Ryanair (www.ryanair.com) – Budget flights from several European cities to Beauvais (BVA).

EasyJet (www.easyjet.com) – Budget-friendly flights from the UK, Italy, and Spain.

Asia & Middle East to Paris

Qatar Airways (www.qatarairways.com) – Flights from Doha with connections from Asia.

Emirates (www.emirates.com) – Direct flights from Dubai.

Singapore Airlines (www.singaporeair.com) – Direct flights from Singapore.

ANA (All Nippon Airways) (www.ana.co.jp) – Flights from Tokyo.

Africa & South America to Paris

Air France – Direct flights from Morocco, South Africa, and Brazil.

LATAM Airlines (www.latamairlines.com) – Flights from Brazil, Argentina, and Chile.

Ethiopian Airlines (www.ethiopianairlines.com) – Flights from Addis Ababa.

3. Getting from the Airport to Disneyland Paris

Once you arrive in **Paris**, there are multiple ways to travel from the airport to **Disneyland Paris (Marne-la-Vallée Chessy station)**.

A. Magical Shuttle (Recommended for Convenience)
From: CDG & ORY

Travel Time: 45–60 minutes

Cost: ~€23 (adults), ~€10 (children)

Booking: www.magicalshuttle.com

Contact: +33 1 64 62 30 03

B. TGV High-Speed Train (Fastest Option from CDG)
From: CDG

Travel Time: ~10 minutes

Cost: €19 – €35

Booking: www.sncf-connect.com

Contact: +33 1 84 94 36 35

C. RER A Train (Best Budget Option from Paris City & Orly)

From: ORY (via Orlyval + RER B to RER A)

Travel Time: ~60 minutes

Cost: €10 – €15

Booking: www.ratp.fr

Contact: +33 1 58 77 18 77

D. Taxi / Private Transfer (Most Expensive but Comfortable)

From: CDG, ORY, BVA

Travel Time: 35–90 minutes

Cost: €70 – €150 (varies by distance & provider)

Booking: Available via hotel concierge, Uber, Bolt

4. Final Travel Tips

Book flights early (3–6 months in advance) for the best prices.
Check visa requirements if traveling internationally.
Use the TGV train from CDG for the fastest transfer.
Consider airport lounges for a comfortable layover experience.
Have emergency contacts saved:

Disneyland Paris Guest Services: +33 1 60 30 60 53

Paris Airport Lost & Found: +33 1 70 36 39 50

By planning ahead and choosing the right flight and airport transfer, you can ensure a **smooth and stress-free** arrival at Disneyland Paris!

Traveling to Disneyland Paris by Train

Taking the train is one of the **fastest and most convenient** ways to reach Disneyland Paris, especially if you're traveling from **Paris, other parts of France, or neighboring European countries**.

A. TGV (High-Speed Train) from Paris to Disneyland Paris

The **TGV InOui** (Train à Grande Vitesse) is the fastest train option, connecting Paris to **Marne-la-Vallée Chessy**, the station located **right outside Disneyland Paris**.

Duration: Around **10 minutes** from Paris Gare de Lyon.

Cost: Starts at **€20 one-way**, but varies based on demand and booking time.

Frequency: Trains run **every 30–60 minutes** during peak hours.

Booking & Contact Information:
Official website: www.sncf-connect.com

SNCF Customer Service: **+33 1 84 94 36 35**

B. RER A (Regional Train) from Paris to Disneyland Paris

The **RER A** suburban train is an affordable and widely used option.

Duration: Around **35–40 minutes** from central Paris.

Cost: **€5 per adult, €2.50 per child (one-way)**.

Route: Take the **RER A** towards **Marne-la-Vallée Chessy**, which is the last stop.

Frequency: Trains run **every 10–15 minutes**.

Booking & Contact Information:
Official RATP Website: www.ratp.fr

RATP Customer Service: **+33 1 58 78 80 00**

C. Eurostar (Train from London to Disneyland Paris)

Direct **Eurostar trains** run between **London St Pancras International** and **Marne-la-Vallée Chessy**.

Duration: **2 hours 45 minutes**.

Cost: Starts from **€50–€250 one-way**, depending on the class and time of booking.

Frequency: Usually **one train per day**, more during peak seasons.

Booking & Contact Information:
Official website: www.eurostar.com

Eurostar Customer Service: **+44 3432 186 186** (UK)

Traveling to Disneyland Paris by Bus

Buses provide a **cheaper alternative** to trains but take longer depending on traffic. They are ideal for **budget travelers and large groups**.

A. Disneyland Paris Express (Official Shuttle from Paris)

The **Disneyland Paris Express** is an **official shuttle** connecting central Paris with Disneyland.

Pick-up points:

Gare du Nord

Opéra

Châtelet

Eiffel Tower

Duration: **1 hour 15 minutes** (subject to traffic).

Cost:

€44 per adult (round-trip)

€35 per child (round-trip)

Extras: Includes **park admission ticket packages** if selected.

Booking & Contact Information:
Official website: www.disneylandparis.com

Disneyland Paris Express Hotline: **+33 1 60 30 60 53**

B. Public Buses from Paris to Disneyland Paris
Bus 19 (from Meaux to Disneyland) – a cheaper local bus option.

Duration: **1 hour 30 minutes**.

Cost: **€2 per trip**, covered by a Navigo pass.

Booking & Contact Information:

Bus schedules: www.transdev-idf.com

Customer service: **+33 9 70 80 96 63**

C. Long-Distance Buses from Other European Cities
If you're traveling from other parts of Europe, several **budget-friendly coach companies** operate routes to Disneyland Paris.

Bus Operator	Departing Cities	Estimated Cost	Duration
FlixBus	Brussels, London, Amsterdam, Lyon	€10 – €50	3–8 hours
Ouibus (BlaBlaCar Bus)	Lille, Bordeaux, Marseille	€15 – €40	3–10 hours

Booking & Contact Information:

FlixBus: www.flixbus.com | Customer Service: **+49 30 300137300**

BlaBlaCar Bus: www.blablacar.fr/bus | Customer Service: **+33 1 70 96 86 60**

Driving to Disneyland Paris

Driving is **a flexible and comfortable option**, especially for families or those bringing extra luggage. However, parking fees and **Parisian traffic** can be a concern.

A. Routes to Disneyland Paris

From Paris: Take the **A4 motorway (Autoroute de l'Est)** towards **Metz/Nancy**, then exit at **Sortie 14 – Disneyland Paris**.

From Charles de Gaulle Airport (CDG): Follow the **A104**, then merge onto the **A4** towards Disneyland.

From Orly Airport: Take the **A86** then merge onto the **A4** motorway.

B. Estimated Driving Times

Departure Point	Estimated Time
Paris city center	**40 minutes**
Charles de Gaulle Airport (CDG)	**30 minutes**
Orly Airport (ORY)	**45 minutes**
Lille, France	**2 hours 30 minutes**
Brussels, Belgium	**3 hours**

C. Parking at Disneyland Paris

On-Site Parking: €30 per day for standard vehicles.

Hotel Parking: Free for **Disney hotel guests**.

Val d'Europe Parking (Alternative): €10 per day.

D. Rental Cars

If you need to rent a car, several agencies operate at **CDG Airport, Orly Airport, and central Paris.**

Car Rental Company	Starting Price (Per Day)	Contact Info
Hertz	€40 – €100	www.hertz.com
Avis	€35 – €90	www.avis.fr
Sixt	€45 – €120	www.sixt.fr

Final Tips for Choosing the Best Transportation Option

If you **want speed**, take the **TGV train (10 minutes from Paris)**.

If you're **on a budget**, take the **RER A train** (€5) or a public bus.

If you're **traveling from London**, **Eurostar** is the best option.

If you **prefer convenience**, **Disneyland Express** shuttle buses are great.

If you're **traveling with a group**, consider renting a car.

From Paris to Disneyland Paris: Transportation Guide

Disneyland Paris is located in **Marne-la-Vallée**, about **32 km (20 miles) east of Paris**. Whether you're traveling from central Paris, Charles de Gaulle Airport (CDG), Orly Airport (ORY), or other surrounding areas, multiple transportation options are available. This guide provides a **detailed breakdown of all travel methods**, including costs, durations, schedules, and contact details where applicable.

1. By Train (RER A) – The Fastest and Most Convenient Option

The **RER A regional train** is the most **affordable and efficient** way to get to Disneyland Paris from the city center.

Key Details

Departure Stations in Paris:

Charles de Gaulle – Étoile

Auber

Châtelet–Les Halles (Major connection hub)

Gare de Lyon (Best for travelers with luggage)

Nation

Arrival Station: Marne-la-Vallée – Chessy (2-minute walk from the Disneyland entrance)

Duration: Approx. **35–45 minutes**

Frequency: Every **10–15 minutes**

Operating Hours: 5:30 AM – 12:30 AM

Cost: €5 – €10 (one-way)

How to Buy Tickets
Ticket Machines & Booths: Available at RER and metro stations.

Online: Purchase via the official **Île-de-France Mobilités** website (www.iledefrance-mobilites.fr).

Mobile App: Use apps like **Bonjour RATP** for ticket purchases and real-time schedules.

Contact Information
RATP (Paris Transport Authority) |+33 1 58 78 80 00|www.ratp.fr

Tip: If you're staying in Paris for multiple days, consider a **Navigo Pass** for unlimited travel, including RER and metro rides.

2. By High-Speed Train (TGV) – The Fastest Option from Other Cities

If you're arriving from another **French city** or **neighboring European countries**, the **TGV (Train à Grande Vitesse)** offers the **fastest** way to Disneyland Paris.

Key Details

Departure Station in Paris: Gare de Lyon

Arrival Station: Marne-la-Vallée – Chessy TGV Station (Inside Disneyland Paris)

Duration: 10 minutes from Gare de Lyon

Frequency: Every **30–60 minutes**

Cost: €20 – €40 (one-way, depending on demand)

How to Buy Tickets

Online: Purchase via the **SNCF website** (www.sncf-connect.com).

App: Download **SNCF Connect** for booking and schedules.

Contact Information

SNCF Customer Service | +33 8 92 35 35 35| www.sncf-connect.com

Tip: Book in advance for cheaper fares, especially during peak travel seasons.

3. By Bus – The Budget Option

Several bus companies operate **direct shuttle services** between Paris and Disneyland Paris. This is a **cheaper alternative** but takes longer than the train.

A. Disneyland Express Shuttle (Best for Tourists)

Departure Points:

Gare du Nord

Opéra

Châtelet

Duration: 60–90 minutes (depends on traffic)

Cost: €23 (one-way), €29 (round trip)

Tickets: Book online via www.disneylandparis.com

B. Public Bus (Line 19 or 34 from Nearby Towns)

Cheapest option but **not recommended** for first-time visitors as it requires transfers.

Duration: Up to 2 hours with connections.

Fare: €2 – €5 per ride.

Tip: If traveling with kids or large luggage, a train or taxi is more comfortable than a bus.

4. By Taxi – The Comfortable but Expensive Option

Taxis provide a **direct, hassle-free** ride but are significantly **more expensive** than public transport.

Key Details

Pickup Location: Any location in Paris, including hotels and airports.

Drop-off Location: Disneyland Paris main entrance or hotel.

Duration: 45–60 minutes (varies with traffic).

Cost:

From central Paris: €70 – €100

From Charles de Gaulle Airport: €80 – €120

From Orly Airport: €90 – €130

Recommended Taxi Services

G7 Taxis

+33 1 47 39 47 39|www.g7.fr

Taxis Bleus

+33 1 49 36 10 10|www.taxis-bleus.com

Tip: Always **confirm the fare before starting the ride** and ensure the taxi is licensed.

5. By Ride-Sharing (Uber, Bolt, Kapten) – A More Affordable Alternative to Taxis

Ride-sharing apps like **Uber** and **Bolt** offer a more **budget-friendly alternative** to taxis. Prices **fluctuate** based on demand and time of day.

Estimated Costs

Ride Type	Cost from Paris	Cost from CDG Airport
UberX	€50 – €80	€55 – €90
Uber Comfort	€70 – €100	€80 – €120
Uber Van (6-seater)	€80 – €130	€90 – €150

Tip: Check the fare estimate on the app before confirming a ride.

6. By Rental Car – Best for Flexible Travel

If you prefer **flexibility**, renting a car may be a good option, especially for **families** or those exploring beyond Disneyland Paris.

Key Details

Driving Distance: 45 minutes from Paris.

Parking Fee at Disneyland: €30 per day.

Rental Cost: €50 – €100 per day (varies by car type).

Recommended Rental Companies
Hertz: www.hertz.com

Europcar: www.europcar.com

Avis: www.avis.com

Tip: Rent a car **only if you plan to visit other locations**, as parking is expensive.

Chapter 3

Tickets & Packages

Ticket Types and Prices

Disneyland Paris offers a variety of **ticket options** to suit different budgets and visit preferences. Whether you're planning a **single-day visit** or an **extended stay**, choosing the right ticket can help you **save money** and maximize your experience. Below is a **detailed guide** to Disneyland Paris ticket types, pricing, discounts, and where to buy them.

1. Standard 1-Day Tickets (Dated & Undated)

1-day tickets are ideal for visitors who plan to experience Disneyland Paris for a **single day**. There are two types:

A. Dated Ticket (Best for Cheaper Prices & Guaranteed Entry)

This ticket is valid **only on the selected date**.

Prices **vary depending on the season and expected crowd levels**.

Offers the **lowest price** compared to other single-day tickets.

Guaranteed entry, even on busy days.

Pricing (Per Person) – 2025 Estimates

Park Access	Adults (12+)	Children (3-11)
1 Park, Low Season	€56 – €70	€52 – €65
1 Park, High Season	€75 – €99	€70 – €95
2 Parks, Low Season	€81 – €94	€76 – €89
2 Parks, High Season	€94 – €124	€89 – €119

Where to Buy:

Official Disneyland Paris Website: www.disneylandparis.com

Official Disneyland Paris App (iOS & Android)

Authorized ticket resellers (e.g., Fnac, GetYourGuide)

Tip: Book in advance to secure lower prices. Prices increase closer to the date.

B. Undated Ticket (Flexible but More Expensive)

Allows entry on **any day** within **one year** from the purchase date.

Recommended if you are unsure of your exact visit date.

More **expensive than dated tickets** because of flexibility.

Pricing (Per Person) – 2025 Estimates

Park Access	Adults (12+)	Children (3-11)
1 Park, Any Day	€109	€100
2 Parks, Any Day	€134	€124

Where to Buy:

Official Disneyland Paris Website/App

Disney Stores & Travel Agencies

Tip: Only buy an **undated ticket** if you need flexibility, as it costs more than a dated ticket.

2. Multi-Day Tickets (Best for Longer Visits & Savings)

If you plan to spend **two or more days** at Disneyland Paris, a **multi-day ticket** is the best option. It provides **cheaper per-day pricing** compared to buying single-day tickets.

Pricing (Per Person) – 2025 Estimates

Days	2 Parks Access	Adults (12+)	Children (3-11)
2 Days	Yes	€166	€152
3 Days	Yes	€222	€205
4 Days	Yes	€259	€235

Where to Buy:
Disneyland Paris Website/App

Disneyland Paris Ticket Booths

Tip: The **4-day ticket** offers the **best value per day** if you want the full Disney experience.

3. Disneyland Paris Annual Pass (For Frequent Visitors)

For guests who visit **multiple times per year**, an **Annual Pass** provides **unlimited access** and **exclusive benefits** like discounts on food, merchandise, and hotel stays. There are four types of annual passes:

Annual Pass Type	Price	Park Access	Blockout Dates	Discounts & Perks
Bronze Pass	€289	Both Parks	150+ Days	-
Silver Pass	€499	Both Parks	100+ Days	Up to **10% off** restaurants & shops
Gold Pass	€699	Both Parks	Few Blockout Days	**15% off** restaurants & shops, free parking

Annual Pass Type	Price	Park Access	Blockout Dates	Discounts & Perks
Infinity Pass	€999	Both Parks	No Blockout Dates	20% off restaurants & shops, VIP areas, free parking

Where to Buy:

Online: www.disneylandparis.com

At the Park: Ticket booths at Disneyland Paris entrance.

Tip: If you plan to visit at least **three times per year**, an **Annual Pass** saves money.

4. Discounted Tickets & Special Offers

Disneyland Paris regularly offers **discounts** and **special deals** for visitors.

A. Special Discounts

Children Under 3: Free entry
Children Aged 3-11: Reduced rates
Disabled Guests: Discounted rates (Contact Disney customer service)
Military Discounts: Available for service members (Check with ID)

Where to Find Discounts:

Disneyland Paris Promotions Page: www.disneylandparis.com/en-gb/offers

Authorized Resellers (Fnac, Cdiscount, GetYourGuide)

Tip: Sign up for Disney emails to receive alerts on ticket sales and exclusive offers.

5. VIP & Special Experience Tickets

For guests who want a **luxury experience**, Disneyland Paris offers **VIP experiences** with exclusive access to attractions.

A. Disney Premier Access (Skip-the-Line Pass)

What It Does: Allows you to **skip the regular queues** for select rides.

Price: Starts at **€5 – €18 per ride**, varies by attraction.

Where to Buy: Disneyland Paris App or in-park kiosks.

Tip: Buy a **Premier Access Pass** on busy days to save time on long queues.

B. Disneyland Paris VIP Tours

What It Includes:
Private tour guide
Instant ride access (no waiting)
VIP viewing area for shows & parades

Price: Starts from **€2,500 per group (up to 10 people)**

Booking Contact:
+33 1 60 30 50 60|www.disneylandparis.com

Tip: VIP Tours sell out fast—book at least **1-2 months in advance**.

Annual Passes and Special Offers at Disneyland Paris

Disneyland Paris offers several **Annual Pass options** and **special discounts** that allow visitors to save money while enjoying multiple visits, exclusive perks, and VIP experiences. Whether you're a frequent visitor, a family looking for discounts, or a budget traveler, this guide provides a **detailed breakdown** of all available **passes, discounts, and offers** to help you maximize your Disneyland Paris experience.

Annual Passes at Disneyland Paris

Disneyland Paris **Annual Passes (Pass Annuels)** allow unlimited or semi-unlimited access to the parks throughout the year, along with **exclusive discounts, early access, VIP services, and event invitations**.

1. Types of Annual Passes
A. Bronze Annual Pass (€289)

Best for: Guests who visit during off-peak seasons and don't need extra perks.
Restrictions: Cannot be used on peak dates, holidays, or summer weekends.

B. Silver Annual Pass (€499)

Best for: Frequent visitors who want flexible dates and discounts.
Includes:

Access to **300 days per year**

10% discount on food, merchandise, and hotels

Free parking at Disneyland Paris
Restrictions: Blackout dates apply during **Christmas, New Year, and summer holidays**.

C. Gold Annual Pass (€699)

Best for: Hardcore Disney fans who want unlimited access and exclusive perks.
Includes:

No blackout dates (365 days/year access)

15% discount on food, merchandise, and hotels

Exclusive reserved seating for parades and shows

Extra Magic Hours (early park access before opening)

Free parking

Discounts on special events (Halloween, Christmas parties)

Tip: If you plan to visit **more than 3 times per year**, an **Annual Pass** is **cheaper than buying separate tickets**.

2. How to Buy an Annual Pass

You can purchase Annual Passes:

Online: Via the official Disneyland Paris website (www.disneylandparis.com)

On-Site: At the **Annual Pass Office** inside Disneyland Paris (next to the entrance)

By Phone: +33 1 60 30 60 53

Tip: Check the **official Disneyland Paris website** for **flash sales** on Annual Passes!

Special Offers and Discounts at Disneyland Paris

Disneyland Paris regularly offers **limited-time promotions** and **discounts** for visitors. These offers vary throughout the year and can include:

1. Seasonal Ticket Discounts

Disneyland Paris often **reduces ticket prices** during the **low season** (January – March, September – November). Discounts can go up to **30% off** standard ticket prices.

How to Find Seasonal Discounts?

Check www.disneylandparis.com for current deals.

Subscribe to the **Disneyland Paris newsletter** for exclusive offers.

Tip: Prices **increase** during **school holidays and weekends**, so book in advance!

2. Hotel + Ticket Bundles

Disneyland Paris offers **discounted packages** that include:
Hotel stay at a **Disney Resort**
Park tickets for **all days of stay**
Early park entry

Best Time to Book?

January – March → Cheapest rates

May – June → Moderate rates

December → Highest prices due to Christmas events

Tip: Booking a **Disney hotel package** can save up to **20%** compared to buying tickets and hotels separately.

3. Family and Group Discounts
Kids under 3 → **FREE** entry

Kids under 12 → Often get **reduced ticket prices** in special promotions

Groups of 20+ people → Special rates available (call **+33 1 60 30 60 53** for group bookings)

Tip: Book as a **group** to save **10–15%** on hotel and ticket packages.

4. Annual Pass Discounts on Hotels, Food & Merchandise
If you have a **Silver or Gold Annual Pass**, you can enjoy:
10–15% off Disney hotels
10–15% off **food & drinks** inside the parks
Discounts on special events (e.g., **Halloween, New Year's Eve**)

Tip: Use your **Annual Pass** at **Disney Village restaurants** (outside the park) for discounts.

5. Disney Meal Plan Offers
Disneyland Paris offers **Meal Plans** that include food & drinks at park restaurants at a **discounted rate**.

Meal Plan	Price (€ per day)	Includes
Standard	€39 (adult), €29 (child)	2-course meal + drink
Plus	€59 (adult), €39 (child)	3-course meal + drink
Premium	€79 (adult), €49 (child)	All-you-can-eat buffets

Tip: If you plan to eat **3+ meals inside the park**, a Meal Plan can save you **€10–€15 per person daily**.

6. Discounted Tickets for Residents & Students

Disneyland Paris sometimes offers **special discounts for French residents** and **European students**.

Île-de-France residents → 10% off select tickets

Students (under 26) → **Reduced rates** during off-peak days

Tip: Bring a valid **student ID** to claim discounts at the ticket counter.

7. Free Entry on Your Birthday (Limited-Time Offer)

Disneyland Paris **occasionally** offers **free entry** for guests celebrating their birthday! 🎉

Available for: Guests visiting on their **exact birth date**
How to Redeem: Bring a **valid ID** and check at the ticket booth.

Tip: Call customer service to confirm if this **offer is available** during your visit.

Final Recommendations

Best Option	Who Should Choose It?
Bronze Annual Pass (€289)	Budget travelers visiting **3+ times a year**.
Silver Annual Pass (€499)	Frequent visitors who want **discounts & parking perks**.
Gold Annual Pass (€699)	Disney lovers who want **unlimited VIP access & extra perks**.
Seasonal Ticket Discounts	Visitors traveling **off-peak (January-March, September-November)**.
Hotel + Ticket Bundles	Families looking for **convenience & early park entry**.
Group Discounts	Groups of **20+ people** booking together.

Chapter 4

Accommodation

Finding the right accommodation is an important part of planning your trip to Disneyland Paris. The park offers **official Disney hotels, nearby partner hotels**, and a variety of **budget and luxury options** to suit different preferences and budgets. Staying at an **official Disney hotel** provides exclusive benefits such as **Extra Magic Hours (early park access), free shuttle services, character meet-and-greets, and immersive Disney themes**. However, **partner hotels and budget-friendly accommodations** near Disneyland Paris can be a great alternative for those looking to save money while still being close to the magic. Below is a detailed breakdown of the available options.

Official Disneyland Paris Hotels

Disneyland Paris features **six official Disney hotels**, each offering a unique theme and experience. These hotels are located **either within walking distance or a short shuttle ride from the parks**, making them the most convenient choices for visitors who want to stay close to the action.

Disneyland Hotel (★★★★★) – Ultimate Luxury Experience

The **Disneyland Hotel** is the most prestigious and luxurious hotel in Disneyland Paris. Located **right at the entrance of Disneyland Park**, this **Victorian-style** hotel provides a **5-star experience** with stunning architecture, high-end dining, and personalized Disney services. Guests staying here enjoy **VIP treatment, exclusive park views, fine dining, and character dining experiences**. The hotel also features a **spa, an indoor swimming pool, and concierge services** for a truly extravagant stay.

Location: Directly at the entrance of Disneyland Park
Contact: +33 1 60 45 65 00
Price Range: From €800 per night

This hotel is best suited for those who want **the most exclusive Disney experience** with direct park access, premium services, and a fairy-tale atmosphere. However, it comes with a **high price tag**, making it ideal for luxury travelers and special occasions.

Disney's Hotel New York – The Art of Marvel (★★★★) – A Superhero Stay

For Marvel fans, **Disney's Hotel New York – The Art of Marvel** is the perfect choice. This **four-star hotel**, located **just a 10-minute walk or short shuttle ride from the parks**, is decorated with over **350 pieces of**

Marvel artwork, offering an immersive experience for comic book lovers. Guests can enjoy **Marvel-themed rooms, a Hero Training Center with a Spider-Man meet-and-greet, and stylish lounges inspired by New York City**.

Location: 10-minute walk or free shuttle from the parks
Contact: +33 1 60 45 73 00
Price Range: From €450 per night

This hotel is great for those who love **modern designs, luxury amenities, and Marvel characters**. It also features an **indoor pool, a fitness center, and stylish dining options**, making it an exciting yet sophisticated stay.

Disney's Newport Bay Club (★★★★) – Nautical Elegance

For guests who prefer a **seaside-inspired** theme, **Disney's Newport Bay Club** offers a **New England coastal resort** ambiance. This **four-star hotel** is just **a 15-minute walk from Disneyland Paris or a short shuttle ride away**. The hotel features **maritime decor, elegant rooms, and a lakeside setting** that provides a tranquil atmosphere. Guests can also enjoy **indoor and outdoor swimming pools, a fitness center, and a premium restaurant**.

Location: 15-minute walk or free shuttle from the parks
Contact: +33 1 60 45 55 00
Price Range: From €350 per night

This hotel is perfect for **families and couples** who want a **peaceful retreat** with Disney charm. It offers a **high-end experience without the premium price of Disneyland Hotel.**

Disney's Sequoia Lodge (★★★) – Cozy Wilderness Retreat

For those who love nature and a **cozy, rustic atmosphere**, **Disney's Sequoia Lodge** is a great option. Inspired by **U.S. National Park lodges**, this hotel features **wooden interiors, warm fireplaces, and a relaxing environment**. Located **a 15-minute walk from Disneyland Paris**, the hotel provides **a comfortable stay with an indoor pool, a hot tub, and a welcoming lounge area.**

Location: 15-minute walk or free shuttle from the parks
Contact: +33 1 60 45 51 00
Price Range: From €250 per night

This hotel is best suited for **families and nature lovers** looking for a **mid-range hotel with a calm and cozy atmosphere.**

Disney's Hotel Cheyenne (★★★) – Wild West Adventure

For visitors who love **cowboy and Western themes**, **Disney's Hotel Cheyenne** offers a fun and immersive experience. The hotel is **styled like an Old West town**, with **rooms featuring Toy Story's Woody and Jessie**. The hotel is **one of the more affordable Disney options**, making it a great choice for families on a budget.

Location: 20-minute walk or free shuttle from the parks
Contact: +33 1 60 45 62 00
Price Range: From €200 per night

This hotel is best for **families with young kids** who love **a playful, Western-inspired atmosphere at a reasonable price**.

Disney's Hotel Santa Fe (★★) – Budget-Friendly Cars-Themed Hotel

For the most budget-friendly option inside Disneyland Paris, **Disney's Hotel Santa Fe** is a great choice. This hotel has a **Cars movie theme**, featuring **desert-inspired decor and colorful Pixar touches**. While it is a **two-star hotel**, it still offers the benefits of a Disney hotel, including **free shuttle service and early park access**.

Location: 20-minute walk or free shuttle from the parks
Contact: +33 1 60 45 78 00
Price Range: From €180 per night

This is the **most affordable official Disney hotel**, making it ideal for **budget-conscious families** who still want to enjoy Disney perks.

Nearby Partner Hotels

If staying at a **Disney hotel** is not within your budget or you prefer alternative options, Disneyland Paris has a selection of **partner hotels** located within a short distance of the parks. These hotels are **officially affiliated** with Disneyland Paris, offering **shuttle services** to and from the parks, and often provide more affordable rates than Disney-owned accommodations.

Here are some of the top nearby partner hotels:
1. B&B Hôtel Disneyland Paris

Location: 60 Avenue de la Fosse des Pressoirs, 77700 Magny-le-Hongre, France
Contact: +33 1 64 17 90 00
Price Range: €70 – €130 per night

This budget-friendly hotel offers **clean, modern rooms**, a **free shuttle service** to Disneyland Paris, and a **continental breakfast buffet**. It's an excellent choice for travelers looking for affordability without sacrificing convenience.

2. Campanile Val de France (Formerly Kyriad Hotel Disneyland Paris)

Location: 10 Avenue de la Fosse des Pressoirs, 77700 Magny-le-Hongre, France
Contact: +33 1 60 43 61 61
Price Range: €80 – €140 per night

A comfortable, family-friendly hotel with **spacious rooms**, an **on-site restaurant**, and a **shuttle service** to the parks. The hotel also features a small **farm with animals**, making it a great option for families with children.

3. Explorers Hotel

Location: 50 Avenue de la Fosse des Pressoirs, 77700 Magny-le-Hongre, France
Contact: +33 1 60 42 60 00
Price Range: €120 – €180 per night

A themed hotel designed for families, featuring **pirate-themed rooms**, an **indoor water playground**, and multiple dining options. It's perfect for families looking for fun even outside the parks.

4. Radisson Blu Hotel Paris, Marne-la-Vallée

Location: Allée de la Mare Houleuse, 77700 Magny-le-Hongre, France
Contact: +33 1 60 43 64 00
Price Range: €150 – €250 per night

A high-end hotel offering **spacious, elegant rooms**, a **spa**, an **indoor swimming pool**, and a **golf course** nearby. This is a great option for those seeking a more relaxing stay with upscale amenities while still being close to Disneyland Paris.

5. Adagio Marne-la-Vallée Val d'Europe

Location: 42 Cours du Danube, 77700 Serris, France
Contact: +33 1 64 17 32 00
Price Range: €90 – €160 per night

This **aparthotel** is ideal for families and groups who want to stay in a **self-catering apartment** with a kitchen. Located near **Val d'Europe shopping mall**, it offers great accessibility to both Disneyland Paris and shopping/dining options.

Budget vs. Luxury Options

Your choice of accommodation depends on your **budget, preferences, and the kind of experience you want**. Here's a detailed breakdown of **budget-friendly** and **luxury** accommodation options near Disneyland Paris.

Budget Hotels (Under €150 per night)

If you're traveling on a budget, there are several affordable hotels that provide a **comfortable stay without high costs**.

Best for: Solo travelers, backpackers, or families looking to save money

Common Features: Basic rooms, free WiFi, breakfast available, and shuttle service to Disneyland Paris

Top Choices:

B&B Hôtel Disneyland Paris – Best for budget-conscious travelers with simple but comfortable rooms

Campanile Val de France – Great for families with an **on-site restaurant** and kids' play area

Adagio Marne-la-Vallée Val d'Europe – Best for groups who want apartment-style stays

Tip: Book at least **3-4 months in advance** to get the lowest prices. Prices increase during school holidays and weekends.

Mid-Range Hotels (€150 – €300 per night)

If you want **extra comfort** while still maintaining affordability, mid-range hotels offer **better amenities** like pools, larger rooms, and on-site dining options.

Best for: Families, couples, and travelers who want a **balance of comfort and affordability**

Common Features: Bigger rooms, pools, restaurants, and spa services

Top Choices:

Explorers Hotel – Best for families with kids, offering **indoor water slides** and themed rooms

Radisson Blu Hotel – Perfect for couples and business travelers, featuring **a spa and elegant design**

Tip: Look for **seasonal promotions** where these hotels offer free breakfast or discounts on park tickets.

Luxury Hotels (€300+ per night)

For visitors who want a **high-end Disney experience**, luxury hotels offer **premium services, stunning designs, and VIP treatment**.

Best for: Couples on a romantic trip, Disney superfans, or those looking for the **ultimate Disney stay**

Common Features: Elegant suites, private dining, spa facilities, and premium park access

Top Choices:

Disneyland Hotel (Reopening in 2024) – **The most luxurious Disney hotel,** located **right at the entrance**

of **Disneyland Park**, with **5-star service and character dining**

Hotel New York – The Art of Marvel – A high-end, **Marvel-themed hotel**, offering immersive experiences, luxury rooms, and a unique art gallery

Disney's Newport Bay Club – A 4-star, **Nautical-themed hotel**, known for **excellent service and beautiful lake views**

Tip: If you want to **maximize your Disney experience**, luxury hotels offer **Extra Magic Time**, allowing guests to **enter the park before opening hours**.

Chapter 5

Parks Overview

Disneyland Paris is home to **two distinct theme parks**: **Disneyland Park**, which is the main and most iconic park, and **Walt Disney Studios Park**, which focuses on movies, animation, and behind-the-scenes experiences. Each park offers unique attractions, entertainment, and immersive theming. Understanding the differences between these parks will help visitors **plan their visit effectively**, prioritize attractions, and maximize their experience.

Disneyland Park

Location: Disneyland Paris, Boulevard de Parc, 77700 Coupvray, France
Opening Hours: Typically **9:30 AM – 11:00 PM** (hours may vary by season)
Tickets: Included in all Disneyland Paris ticket options

Disneyland Park is the **flagship park** of Disneyland Paris and is modeled after the original **Disneyland in California** and **Magic Kingdom in Florida**. It is a **fairy-tale-inspired park** that transports visitors into a world of classic Disney storytelling. The park is divided into **five themed lands**, each with **unique attractions, dining, and entertainment**.

1. Main Street, U.S.A.

Main Street, U.S.A. is the **entrance to Disneyland Park**, designed to resemble a **turn-of-the-century American town** inspired by Walt Disney's childhood.

Key Highlights:

Spectacular view of Sleeping Beauty Castle

Disneyland Railroad – Take a scenic train ride around the park

Restaurants & Shops – Includes **Walt's – An American Restaurant** and souvenir shops

Parades & Nighttime Shows – The **Disney Stars on Parade** and **Disney Dreams nighttime fireworks show**

2. Fantasyland

Fantasyland is where **classic Disney fairy tales come to life**, making it the most **magical and family-friendly area** of the park.

Key Attractions:

Sleeping Beauty Castle (Le Château de la Belle au Bois Dormant) – The park's iconic centerpiece with a **dragon animatronic** in the dungeon

It's a Small World – A classic Disney boat ride with animatronic dolls singing about world unity

Peter Pan's Flight – A magical flying ride over **Neverland**

Alice's Curious Labyrinth – A walk-through maze based on *Alice in Wonderland*

3. Adventureland

Adventureland is themed around **exotic jungles, pirate adventures, and ancient ruins**, appealing to thrill-seekers and explorers.

Key Attractions:

Pirates of the Caribbean – A legendary boat ride featuring Captain Jack Sparrow and epic pirate battles

Indiana Jones and the Temple of Peril – A high-speed **roller coaster** through an ancient temple

Adventure Isle & Skull Rock – A playground and exploration area inspired by **Treasure Island**

4. Frontierland

Frontierland is **Western-themed**, bringing visitors into the world of cowboys, gold mines, and ghost towns.

Key Attractions:

Big Thunder Mountain – A thrilling mine train roller coaster set in the Wild West

Phantom Manor – Disneyland Paris's unique version of the Haunted Mansion, with a **mysterious and darker storyline**

Thunder Mesa Riverboat Landing – A relaxing **paddlewheel boat ride** around Frontierland

5. Discoveryland

Discoveryland is Disneyland Paris's **version of Tomorrowland**, inspired by futuristic exploration and **Jules Verne-style adventure**.

Key Attractions:

Star Wars Hyperspace Mountain – A high-speed indoor roller coaster with a **Star Wars** theme

Buzz Lightyear Laser Blast – An interactive ride where you help **Buzz Lightyear defeat Zurg**

Autopia – A driving attraction for kids in futuristic cars

Walt Disney Studios Park

Location: Adjacent to Disneyland Park, Disneyland Paris

Opening Hours: Typically **9:30 AM – 9:00 PM** (varies by season)

Tickets: Included in multi-park tickets or **can be visited separately**

Walt Disney Studios Park is **dedicated to the magic of film, television, and animation**. It offers **behind-the-scenes experiences**, **movie-themed attractions**, and **thrilling rides**. The park is undergoing **major expansion**, with new lands based on *Frozen*, *Marvel*, and *Star Wars* set to open in the coming years.

1. Front Lot

This is the entrance to Walt Disney Studios Park, designed to resemble **classic Hollywood in its golden age**.

Key Highlights:

Studio 1 – A Hollywood-style boulevard with shops and restaurants

Meet Disney Characters – Frequent appearances from Mickey, Minnie, and Goofy in **Hollywood costumes**

2. Avengers Campus (Marvel-Themed Land)

This newly opened **Marvel land** brings the world of superheroes to life, featuring **immersive rides, live-action shows, and character meet-and-greets**.

Key Attractions:

Spider-Man W.E.B. Adventure – A **motion-based interactive ride** where guests help Spider-Man stop rogue spider-bots

Avengers Assemble: Flight Force – A **high-speed roller coaster** featuring **Iron Man and Captain Marvel**

Pym Kitchen – A unique Marvel-themed restaurant with **giant and tiny food portions**

3. Worlds of Pixar

A vibrant land based on popular **Pixar movies**, featuring attractions from *Ratatouille, Toy Story, Finding Nemo*, and more.

Key Attractions:

Ratatouille: The Adventure – A 4D ride through **Gusteau's restaurant** from *Ratatouille*

RC Racer – A **high-speed half-pipe coaster** themed around *Toy Story*

Crush's Coaster – A **spinning roller coaster** based on *Finding Nemo*, one of the park's most popular rides

4. Production Courtyard

A tribute to **Hollywood and filmmaking**, this area features behind-the-scenes experiences and thrilling attractions.

Key Attractions:

The Twilight Zone Tower of Terror – A **drop tower ride** based on the *Twilight Zone* TV series, with a creepy, haunted storyline

CinéMagique – A tribute to the **history of cinema**, blending live-action performances and classic movie clips

Upcoming Expansions (2025 & Beyond)

Disney is expanding Walt Disney Studios Park with **new themed areas**, including:

Frozen Land – Featuring **Arendelle Castle, a boat ride, and character experiences**

Star Wars Land (Rumored) – A possible **Star Wars-themed expansion**

Lakeside Area – A new central area with **gardens, restaurants, and entertainment spaces**

Which Park Should You Visit?

For Classic Disney Magic: Disneyland Park is the best choice, offering **iconic attractions and fairy-tale experiences**.

For Movie Fans & Thrill-Seekers: Walt Disney Studios Park is perfect for **Marvel, Pixar, and Hollywood-themed rides**.

For Families with Young Kids: Disneyland Park (Fantasyland) is the most kid-friendly with gentle rides and meet-and-greets.

For Adrenaline Junkies: Walt Disney Studios Park has the most **thrilling rides**, including **Tower of Terror** and **Flight Force**.

Tip: If you have **only one day**, focus on **Disneyland Park**. If you have **two or more days**, visit **both parks** for a complete experience.

Chapter 6

Disneyland Park – Main Attractions & Lands

Main Street, U.S.A.

Location: The entrance to Disneyland Park, Disneyland Paris

Opening Hours: Matches Disneyland Park opening hours (typically **9:30 AM – 11:00 PM**)

Access: Included with all Disneyland Paris tickets

Main Street, U.S.A. is the **gateway to Disneyland Park**, designed to resemble a **turn-of-the-century American town** inspired by **Walt Disney's childhood in Marceline, Missouri**. The land captures the charm of early **20th-century America**, with its **Victorian architecture, vintage vehicles, street performances, shops, and restaurants.**

As soon as guests pass through the **Disneyland Railroad Station**, they step into an immersive world where nostalgic music plays, cast members wear period costumes, and the street is lined with buildings that house boutiques, restaurants, and even a hidden apartment above one of the shops.

Key Features & Experiences
A Stunning View of Sleeping Beauty Castle

One of the most magical moments at Disneyland Paris is the **first glimpse of Sleeping Beauty Castle (Le Château de la Belle au Bois Dormant)** at the end of Main Street, U.S.A. The castle serves as the park's **centerpiece** and acts as a transition from the real world into the fantasy worlds of Disneyland.

Tip: For a unique perspective, stand under the **arcades on either side of Main Street** for an **unobstructed view** without the crowds.

Main Street Transportation
Main Street, U.S.A. offers various **vintage transportation options**, allowing guests to travel in style from **Town Square** at the entrance to **Central Plaza**, near Sleeping Beauty Castle. These vehicles add to the charm and atmosphere of early 20th-century America.

Disneyland Railroad
What it is: A scenic train ride that **circles the entire park**, with stops in **Frontierland, Fantasyland, and Discoveryland.**

Why ride it? A great way to rest while enjoying **beautiful park views.**

Location: Board at Main Street Station (above the park entrance).

Horse-Drawn Streetcars

What it is: Elegant streetcars pulled by horses offer a **slow and charming ride** down Main Street.

Why ride it? Ideal for soaking in the **atmosphere** and taking unique photos.

Vintage Cars & Omnibus

What it is: Guests can board a **classic 1920s vehicle** or a **double-decker omnibus** to ride along Main Street.

Why ride it? A great way to experience the park **from an elevated view.**

Tip: These vehicles operate **only in the morning** and during **off-peak hours**, so ride early!

Entertainment & Special Events

Disney Stars on Parade

Time: Usually in the **afternoon** (check the Disneyland Paris app for daily schedules).

What to expect: A spectacular procession of Disney characters, themed floats, dancers, and music.

Best Viewing Spots:

Near Town Square (Entrance) → Less crowded, great for photos.

Central Plaza (Near Sleeping Beauty Castle) → Best for **immersive views**.

Disney Dreams Nighttime Fireworks Show

Time: Right before park closing.

What to expect: A breathtaking **fireworks, light, and water projection show on Sleeping Beauty Castle.**

Best Viewing Spots:

Main Street, U.S.A. (midway down the street) → Less crowded, clear castle view.

Central Plaza (close to the castle) → Best for an **immersive experience** but gets crowded.

Tip: Arrive **30-45 minutes early** for the best viewing spot.

Shopping on Main Street, U.S.A.
Main Street, U.S.A. is the **best place to shop** for souvenirs, collectibles, and Disney-themed merchandise. The stores are designed to **look like vintage boutiques**, and some even have hidden details, like **references to Walt Disney and early animation history.**

Best Shops to Visit

Emporium
What it sells: The **largest shop in Disneyland Paris**, offering **plush toys, clothing, collectibles, and souvenirs**.

Harrington's Fine China & Porcelains
What it sells: Elegant **Disney-themed home decor, fine china, and glass figurines**.

Disney Clothiers, Ltd.
What it sells: Stylish **Disney-themed apparel**, including exclusive Paris designs.

Main Street Jewelers
What it sells: Disney-themed jewelry and watches, including limited-edition items.

Tip: Some shops **close earlier than the park**—shop before the fireworks!

Dining on Main Street, U.S.A.

Main Street, U.S.A. offers a variety of **dining options**, from **quick snacks** to **full-service meals** in beautifully themed restaurants.

Best Restaurants on Main Street

Walt's – An American Restaurant (Fine Dining)
Cuisine: French-American gourmet cuisine

Theme: A tribute to Walt Disney, with rooms inspired by different Disney park lands.

Must-try dish: Filet de Bœuf (Beef Filet) & Walt's Signature Dessert

Casey's Corner (Quick Service)
Cuisine: American-style **hot dogs, fries, and soft drinks**

Theme: A **baseball-themed diner**, inspired by *Casey at the Bat*

Market House Deli (Casual Dining)
Cuisine: Sandwiches, pastries, coffee

Must-try: Croque Monsieur (French-style grilled ham and cheese)

Cable Car Bake Shop *(Bakery & Coffee Shop)*

Must-try: Mickey-shaped cookies & éclairs

Tip: Walt's – An American Restaurant requires **reservations**, which can be made via the Disneyland Paris app.

Hidden Details & Secrets
Windows of Main Street – Many shop windows feature **names of Disney Imagineers and executives**, honoring the creators of Disneyland Paris.

The Secret Apartment – Above **Main Street Transportation Co.**, there's a **hidden apartment** where VIP guests have stayed.

Smell of Freshly Baked Cookies – Disney **pumps artificial scents** into the air near bakeries to **enhance immersion**.

Why Main Street, U.S.A. Is Special

It **transports guests to another era** with its **attention to detail, atmosphere, and immersive storytelling**.

It serves as a **hub for transportation, shopping, dining, and entertainment**.

It **sets the stage for the rest of the park**, creating **a magical first and last impression** for visitors.

Tip: As you leave the park at night, **turn back** for a final view of **Sleeping Beauty Castle**, beautifully illuminated with twinkling lights—**the perfect ending to a magical day**!

Frontierland

Location: Disneyland Park, Disneyland Paris
Typical Opening Hours: 9:30 AM – 11:00 PM (may vary)
Access: Included with all Disneyland Park tickets

Frontierland is **one of the five themed lands** in Disneyland Park, **designed to immerse guests in the American Wild West of the 19th century**. This land is heavily inspired by **cowboy culture, ghost towns, Native American heritage, gold mining towns, and frontier legends**.

The entire area is beautifully themed, featuring **rugged canyons, wooden saloons, paddle steamers, and even an abandoned haunted mansion**, making it one of the most **atmospheric lands in the park**. With its combination of **thrilling rides, scenic boat rides, and unique storytelling**, Frontierland appeals to guests of all ages.

Themed Storyline & Design

Frontierland in Disneyland Paris is set in the fictional town of **Thunder Mesa**, a **prosperous Wild West mining town** with a rich history. The **narrative behind Frontierland connects many of its attractions**, making it one of the most **cohesively themed lands in the entire park**.

The town of **Thunder Mesa** was founded during the **Gold Rush**, attracting miners, traders, and adventurers.

The success of **Big Thunder Mining Company** brought wealth to the town, but rumors of a **supernatural curse** surrounding the mines add an eerie mystery.

Many key attractions in this land, including **Big Thunder Mountain and Phantom Manor**, tie into the **lore of Thunder Mesa**, making the land feel like a living, interconnected world.

Major Attractions in Frontierland

Frontierland is home to some of **Disneyland Paris's most famous attractions**, including the **legendary roller coaster Big Thunder Mountain** and the **mysterious Phantom Manor**.

Big Thunder Mountain
The Signature Attraction of Frontierland

Height Requirement: 1.02m (40 inches)
Ride Duration: ~3 minutes
Intensity Level: Moderate thrill ride with sharp turns and fast speeds

Big Thunder Mountain is **the centerpiece of Frontierland and one of the most famous rides in Disneyland Paris**. Unlike other Disney parks where Big Thunder Mountain is **part of a desert canyon**, the Disneyland Paris version is **built on an island in the middle of the Rivers of the Far West**, making it **visually unique and thrillingly immersive**.

Story & Experience:
Guests board a **runaway mine train** operated by the **Big Thunder Mining Company**, which was once

prosperous but is now rumored to be **haunted by supernatural forces**. The ride speeds through **dark tunnels, sharp turns, collapsing mineshafts, and explosive dynamite blasts**, providing **one of the best roller coaster experiences in the park**.

Fun Fact: Unlike its counterparts in the U.S., the Disneyland Paris version is **faster, longer, and more intense**, making it **one of the best versions of Big Thunder Mountain worldwide**.

Phantom Manor
Disneyland Paris's Unique Take on the Haunted Mansion

Height Requirement: None
Ride Duration: ~6 minutes
Intensity Level: Spooky, but not a thrill ride

Phantom Manor is **Disneyland Paris's version of the classic Haunted Mansion** but features **a darker and more mysterious storyline** that ties into **Thunder Mesa's history**.

Story & Experience:
The ride follows the story of **Melanie Ravenswood**, the daughter of **Henry Ravenswood**, a wealthy owner of **Big Thunder Mining Company**. Melanie was **engaged to a local suitor**, but on the night of her wedding, her groom mysteriously disappeared. **Some say a ghostly**

Phantom took him away, while others believe **her father's ghost cursed the manor** to prevent anyone from taking his daughter away.

Guests board **Doom Buggies** and explore the **haunted mansion**, witnessing **Melanie's ghost wandering the halls**, a **phantom wedding reception**, and **skeletal spirits dancing in the grand ballroom**.

The ride ends with a **dramatic encounter with the Phantom**, ensuring **one of the eeriest and most visually stunning haunted house experiences in Disney history**.

Unique to Disneyland Paris: Unlike the **lighthearted, comedic versions of Haunted Mansion in the U.S.**, Phantom Manor has a **more serious, cinematic, and haunting tone**, making it a favorite among **fans of Disney's darker storytelling**.

Thunder Mesa Riverboat Landing
A Relaxing Paddle Steamer Ride on the Rivers of the Far West

Height Requirement: None
Ride Duration: ~15 minutes
Intensity Level: Slow, scenic ride

This attraction allows guests to **board an authentic paddle steamer** and take a **scenic cruise around**

Frontierland, offering beautiful views of **Big Thunder Mountain, the Phantom Manor,** and the **wilderness landscapes.**

Tip: This is a **great way to relax and take photos** of Frontierland while enjoying a peaceful break from thrill rides.

Rustler Roundup Shootin' Gallery (Additional Activity)
🎯 **A fun interactive experience where guests can test their shooting skills at a Western-themed shooting range.**

Additional fee required (€3 per game)

Features **animated targets** that react when hit

Great for **kids and adults looking for extra fun**

Dining in Frontierland
Frontierland offers **some of the best-themed restaurants** in Disneyland Paris, serving **barbecue, Tex-Mex, and American Western-style food**.

Fuente del Oro Restaurante
Mexican cuisine with a Frontierland twist

Specialties: **Tacos, burritos, churros, and frozen margaritas**

Great outdoor seating area with a view of Big Thunder Mountain

The Lucky Nugget Saloon
A classic Wild West saloon with live entertainment

Specialties: **Burgers, ribs, and fried chicken**

Themed after an old Western gold rush bar with a beautifully decorated interior

Silver Spur Steakhouse
The best steakhouse in Disneyland Paris

Specialties: **Grilled steaks, BBQ ribs, and gourmet sides**

Upscale Western decor with a cozy atmosphere

Shopping in Frontierland
Guests can find **Western-themed merchandise, cowboy hats, and souvenirs** in the land's beautifully themed shops.

Thunder Mesa Mercantile Building
A general store with cowboy hats, leather goods, and Wild West souvenirs

The Spirit of Pocahontas Boutique
A shop inspired by Native American culture, selling handcrafted jewelry, dreamcatchers, and themed apparel

Special Entertainment & Seasonal Events

Disney Halloween Festival (October) – **Frontierland is transformed into a spooky ghost town**, with extra decorations, spooky character meet-and-greets, and Halloween-themed snacks.

Christmas in Frontierland (December) – Features **snowfall effects**, **Christmas trees**, and **Western-style holiday decorations**.

Adventureland

Location: Between Frontierland and Fantasyland
Best for: Thrill-seekers, explorers, and pirate lovers
Theme: Exotic jungles, ancient temples, pirate adventures

Adventureland is **designed as a land of exploration and mystery**, drawing inspiration from **tropical islands, Middle Eastern markets, and jungle ruins**. It blends elements of **pirates, explorers, and legendary**

adventures, making it one of the most visually immersive lands in Disneyland Paris.'

Main Attractions
Pirates of the Caribbean

Type: Boat Ride
Wait Time: 15-30 minutes (Varies)
Location: Adventureland (Pirate's Beach Area)

One of the most famous Disney attractions, **Pirates of the Caribbean** takes guests on a **dark boat ride through an elaborate pirate-filled world**. The Disneyland Paris version is **longer and more detailed** than its counterparts in the U.S.

Highlights:
Features **Captain Jack Sparrow** from *Pirates of the Caribbean* films

Includes **lifelike animatronics, special effects, and detailed pirate town scenes**

Ends with a thrilling **waterfall drop** before returning to the port

Fun Fact: The ride **inspired** the *Pirates of the Caribbean* movie franchise, not the other way around!

Indiana Jones and the Temple of Peril

Type: Roller Coaster
Wait Time: 20-45 minutes
Location: Near Adventureland entrance

This **fast-paced roller coaster** is themed around **Indiana Jones' daring archaeological expeditions**. Unlike other Indiana Jones rides in Disney parks, this one features **an outdoor track with a full 360-degree loop**.

Thrills: Sharp turns, high speeds, and an intense loop

Queue Area: Looks like an ancient temple, with jungle ruins and statues

Ride Experience: Short but **intense**, best for adrenaline seekers

Tip: This ride has **height restrictions (1.40m / 4ft 7in)**, so it's not for small children.

Adventure Isle & Skull Rock

Type: Walkthrough & Play Area
Location: Across from Pirates of the Caribbean

Adventure Isle is a **massive exploration area** with **suspension bridges, caves, and waterfalls**, inspired by *Treasure Island*.

Skull Rock: A **giant rock shaped like a skull**, inspired by *Peter Pan*

La Cabane des Robinson: A **Swiss Family Robinson-themed treehouse** with scenic views

Caves & Bridges: Hidden pathways and **swinging rope bridges**

Perfect for families who want a break from rides and prefer **free exploration**.

Dining in Adventureland

Captain Jack's – Restaurant des Pirates

Serves: Caribbean-style seafood & Creole dishes

Ambiance: Inside **Pirates of the Caribbean ride**, candlelit pirate setting

Reservations Recommended ☏ +33 1 60 30 40 50

Hakuna Matata Restaurant

Serves: African & Middle Eastern cuisine

Famous Dish: Spicy chicken skewers with peanut sauce

Quick Service – No reservations needed

Fantasyland

Location: Behind Sleeping Beauty Castle
Best for: Families, children, and classic Disney fans
Theme: Fairy tales, storybook villages, and enchanted castles

Fantasyland is **the heart of Disneyland Paris**, bringing **classic Disney animated films to life**. It is the **most family-friendly land**, with **gentle rides, charming walkthroughs, and character meet-and-greets**.

Main Attractions
Sleeping Beauty Castle (Le Château de la Belle au Bois Dormant)

Type: Walkthrough + Hidden Attraction
Wait Time: None

The most **iconic structure in Disneyland Paris**, Sleeping Beauty Castle is **larger and more detailed** than other Disney castles.

Features:
Fairy tale murals & stained-glass windows inside

La Tanière du Dragon – A hidden **animatronic dragon** in the castle's dungeon

Perfect Photo Spot!

Fun Fact: This is the **only Disney castle with a moving dragon animatronic!**

It's a Small World
Type: Boat Ride
Wait Time: 5-20 minutes

A **gentle boat ride featuring animatronic children** from around the world, **singing in different languages**.

Highlights:
Bright, colorful sets representing different continents

Multilingual version of the famous song

Peaceful and relaxing ride, great for families

Tip: Best enjoyed in **low crowds**, as it gets **repetitive with long waits**.

Peter Pan's Flight
Type: Dark Ride (Flying)
Wait Time: 30-60 minutes (Very Popular!)

A **flying pirate ship ride over London and Neverland**, based on *Peter Pan*.

Ride Features:

Soar over a glowing London skyline

Fly past Captain Hook's ship and mermaids' lagoon

Great for all ages

Tip: Get a FastPass or arrive early, as this ride has one of the longest wait times in Fantasyland.

Alice's Curious Labyrinth

Type: Walkthrough Maze
Wait Time: None

A **hedge maze inspired by** *Alice in Wonderland*, leading to the Queen of Hearts' castle.

Features:
Hidden surprises and interactive elements

A final climb to a scenic viewpoint at the castle

Great for kids and photo opportunities

Tip: Visit in daylight for the best experience.

Dining in Fantasyland

Auberge de Cendrillon (Cinderella's Royal Table)
Fine dining with Disney Princesses

Traditional French cuisine (Escargot, Beef Tenderloin)

Reservations Required +33 1 60 30 40 50

Pizzeria Bella Notte
Casual Italian dining inspired by *Lady and the Tramp*

Best dish: Mickey-shaped pizza

Discoveryland

Location: Disneyland Park, Disneyland Paris
Typical Hours: 9:30 AM – 11:00 PM (varies by season)
Entry: Included in Disneyland Park tickets

Discoveryland is Disneyland Paris's **vision of the future**, blending **science fiction, space travel, and technological wonders**. Unlike Tomorrowland in other Disney parks, which reflects a **corporate and futuristic aesthetic**, Discoveryland draws inspiration from **European science fiction, particularly the works of Jules Verne and Leonardo da Vinci**. This unique theme creates an atmosphere of **adventure, discovery, and imagination**, transporting guests to **a retro-futuristic world filled with space explorations, high-speed thrills, and interactive experiences**.

Key Attractions in Discoveryland

Star Wars Hyperspace Mountain – A High-Speed Space Battle

Ride Type: High-speed indoor roller coaster
Height Requirement: 1.20m (3'11")
Duration: Approx. 2 minutes
Thrill Level: (High)

Star Wars Hyperspace Mountain is a **unique version of Space Mountain**, exclusive to Disneyland Paris. This indoor roller coaster **catapults riders into an epic space battle**, complete with **loops, high-speed turns, and laser effects**, all set within the **Star Wars universe**.

Ride Experience:

Board your **X-wing starfighter** and get launched at high speed into space

Fly through asteroid fields and dodge enemy TIE fighters

Battle alongside **Rebel forces** while **John Williams' iconic Star Wars soundtrack** plays in the background

Tip: Single Rider queue available for a shorter wait time.

Buzz Lightyear Laser Blast – An Interactive Space Adventure

Ride Type: Dark ride, shooting game
Height Requirement: No restrictions (fun for all ages)
Duration: 4 minutes
Thrill Level: (Low)

Buzz Lightyear Laser Blast is an **interactive shooting game**, where riders help **Buzz Lightyear defeat Emperor Zurg** by shooting **Z-shaped targets** throughout the ride.

Ride Experience:

Step inside a **spaceship-inspired ride vehicle**

Use a **laser cannon** to blast targets and earn points

Compete with friends to achieve the **highest score**

Encounter **animatronic Buzz Lightyear and Zurg** along the way

Tip: Aim for the smaller, hidden targets for higher points.

Autopia – Drive into the Retro Future

Ride Type: Outdoor track driving ride
Height Requirement: 0.81m (2'8") for passengers, 1.32m (4'4") for drivers

Duration: 5 minutes
Thrill Level: (Very Low)

Autopia lets guests **drive their own futuristic car** through a scenic track filled with **twists, turns, and tunnels**. The attraction is inspired by **1950s visions of future highways**, featuring neon lights and vintage aesthetics.

Ride Experience:

Drive a small **gas-powered car** along a guided track

Control the **steering and acceleration** while navigating a **futuristic landscape**

Great for **kids learning to "drive"** with their parents

Tip: The **best time to ride is early in the morning** or late at night when wait times are lower.

Les Mystères du Nautilus – Explore Captain Nemo's Submarine

Attraction Type: Walk-through exhibit
Height Requirement: No restrictions
Duration: Self-paced
Thrill Level: (Very Low)

Inspired by **Jules Verne's 20,000 Leagues Under the Sea**, this walk-through attraction takes guests inside **Captain Nemo's submarine, the Nautilus**. It features **detailed steampunk designs, animatronics, and a thrilling giant squid attack scene.**

Highlights:

Walk through **Nemo's personal study, engine room, and sleeping quarters**

See **antique navigation instruments and deep-sea exploration gadgets**

Watch a **giant squid attack through the porthole**

Tip: This is a great **hidden gem** with no queue, making it perfect for a break.

Mickey's PhilharMagic – A 4D Disney Concert Experience

Ride Type: 4D Theater Show
Height Requirement: No restrictions
Duration: 12 minutes
Thrill Level: (Very Low)

Mickey's PhilharMagic is a **3D musical experience** that combines **classic Disney music and animation** with **in-theater effects like wind and water sprays.**

Show Highlights:

Follow **Donald Duck** as he gets caught in a **magical whirlwind of Disney classics**

Features **The Little Mermaid, Aladdin, The Lion King, and Beauty and the Beast**

Stunning **3D visuals** and an immersive **orchestral soundtrack**

Tip: Great for **families** and an excellent way to **rest indoors** while enjoying a **high-quality Disney show.**

Dining in Discoveryland

Café Hyperion (Largest restaurant in Disneyland Paris)
Quick-service dining with **burgers, salads, and vegetarian options**

Features **a large indoor seating area** with occasional **live shows**

Cool Station (Snack Stand)
Offers **churros, ice cream, and drinks**

Buzz Lightyear's Pizza Planet (Occasionally Open)
Serves **pizza, pasta, and galactic-themed snacks**

Shopping in Discoveryland

Constellations
Sells **Star Wars, Buzz Lightyear, and Space Mountain merchandise**

Star Traders
Specializes in **Star Wars collectibles, lightsabers, and themed apparel**

Discoveryland: Unique to Disneyland Paris
Unlike the futuristic **Tomorrowlands** in other Disney parks, Disneyland Paris's Discoveryland is a **homage to European visionaries** like **Jules Verne, Leonardo da Vinci, and H.G. Wells**. The **steampunk and retro-futuristic design** gives it a **distinct identity**, making it one of the most immersive lands in the park.

Fun Fact: Disneyland Paris is the **only Disney park in the world where Space Mountain has loops**.

Best Strategy for Discoveryland
Rope Drop Strategy:

Head to **Star Wars Hyperspace Mountain** first to avoid long waits

Ride **Buzz Lightyear Laser Blast** before queues build up

Afternoon Escape:

Explore **Les Mystères du Nautilus** when other rides are crowded

Enjoy a relaxing show at **Mickey's PhilharMagic**

Evening Magic:

Ride **Hyperspace Mountain at night** for an even more immersive experience

Grab **a snack at Café Hyperion** and watch **Disney Dreams nighttime show**

Chapter 7

Walt Disney Studios Park

Studio 1, Production Courtyard & Avengers Campus

Location: Disneyland Paris, Marne-la-Vallée, France
Opening Hours: Typically **9:30 AM – 9:00 PM** (varies by season)
Entry: Included in Disneyland Paris tickets

Walt Disney Studios Park, the **second theme park at Disneyland Paris**, is dedicated to the **magic of filmmaking, television, and animation**. It offers a behind-the-scenes look at Hollywood-style productions while featuring thrilling rides, immersive lands, and interactive experiences.

Studio 1 & Production Courtyard
Studio 1 – Step into Classic Hollywood

Location: Main entrance area of Walt Disney Studios Park
Experience Type: Themed walkthrough & dining/shopping area

Studio 1 is **the first stop** upon entering Walt Disney Studios Park. It is **designed as a Hollywood soundstage**, recreating the **Golden Age of Hollywood**, complete with neon signs, vintage film sets, and bustling movie scenes.

Key Highlights:

Classic Hollywood Ambiance: Stroll through a **film set-inspired indoor street**, featuring **iconic landmarks like vintage diners, old movie theaters, and neon-lit billboards**.

Themed Restaurants & Shops: Perfect for grabbing a bite and purchasing movie-themed souvenirs.

A Great Photo Spot: The **detailed Hollywood setting** provides an excellent backdrop for pictures.

Where to Eat in Studio 1?

Restaurant en Coulisse
Fast-food style restaurant with burgers, fries, and salads.

Located **inside Studio 1** with movie set decor.

Contact: +33 1 60 30 60 53

Where to Shop in Studio 1?

Studio Store
Sells **Disneyland Paris merchandise, apparel, and souvenirs**.

Features **exclusive Hollywood-themed collectibles**.

Production Courtyard – Lights, Camera, Action!

Location: Center of Walt Disney Studios Park
Theme: Movie production & behind-the-scenes experiences

Production Courtyard is a tribute to **film and television production**, blending **classic movie-making themes with modern blockbusters**.

The Twilight Zone Tower of Terror – A Free-Fall Horror Experience

Ride Type: Drop tower dark ride
Height Requirement: 1.02m (3'4")
Duration: Approx. 3 minutes
Thrill Level: (High)

This **thrilling drop ride** takes guests into **a haunted Hollywood hotel**, where **a mysterious elevator plunges into darkness**. Inspired by **The Twilight Zone**, this attraction offers a mix of **psychological horror, suspense, and high-speed drops**.

Ride Experience:

Step inside the **Hollywood Tower Hotel lobby**, frozen in time since **a mysterious lightning strike in 1939**.

Enter the **service elevator**, where eerie **ghostly presences** await.

Unexpected drops make each ride different – **you never know when you'll fall!**

Tip: Ride this attraction **at night** for an extra eerie experience.

Avengers Campus – Enter the Marvel Universe
Location: Walt Disney Studios Park, Disneyland Paris
Theme: Marvel Superheroes Training Facility

Avengers Campus is **one of the newest and most immersive areas in Disncyland Paris, dedicated to Marvel superheroes.** Designed as a **training ground for new recruits**, it features **thrilling rides, live-action encounters, and interactive experiences.**

Spider-Man W.E.B. Adventure – Become a Web-Slinger!
Ride Type: Interactive dark ride
Height Requirement: No restrictions
Duration: 5 minutes
Thrill Level: (Medium)

This ride lets guests **become Spider-Man** and **shoot webs with their hands** to stop an army of rogue Spider-Bots.

Ride Experience:

Board a **WEB Slinger vehicle** and use **gesture-based motion tracking** to shoot webs.

Aim at **targets and Spider-Bots**, competing for the **highest score**.

Features **Tom Holland as Spider-Man**, guiding recruits through the mission.

Tip: This ride is **best experienced with family or friends** to compete for **the highest score!**

Avengers Assemble: Flight Force – A High-Speed Iron Man & Captain Marvel Coaster

Ride Type: High-speed indoor roller coaster
Height Requirement: 1.20m (3'11")
Duration: Approx. 1.5 minutes
Thrill Level: (Very High)

This **intense roller coaster** is one of the fastest rides at Disneyland Paris. It features **Iron Man and Captain Marvel**, who recruit guests for a high-stakes space mission.

Ride Experience:

High-speed launch from 0 to **92 km/h (57 mph) in seconds**.

Encounter **Iron Man in a fully animated, talking suit**.

Experience **dark turns, twists, and loops** while dodging cosmic threats.

Tip: This ride has **Single Rider and Premier Access** options for shorter wait times.

Heroic Encounters – Meet Marvel Characters
Location: Avengers Campus
Entry: Included with park admission

In **Avengers Campus**, guests can meet **Iron Man, Spider-Man, Black Panther, Thor, and more**. Characters appear throughout the day for **photo opportunities, training sessions, and live-action interactions**.

Tip: Check the **Disneyland Paris app** for **character appearance times**.

Shopping in Avengers Campus
Mission Equipment – The **official Marvel store** in Avengers Campus.

Features **Spider-Man web shooters, Marvel apparel, and collectibles**.

Exclusive **Avengers Campus merchandise** available.

Dining in Avengers Campus

PYM Kitchen (Buffet Restaurant)

Ant-Man-themed buffet with **oversized and mini-sized foods**.

Reservations: Recommended via the **Disneyland Paris app**.

Stark Factory (Quick Service)

Pizza, pasta, and salads in a **Tony Stark-inspired workshop**.

Toy Story Playland – Step into Andy's Backyard

Location: Walt Disney Studios Park, Toon Studio area
Entry: Included in park admission

Toy Story Playland **shrinks guests down to the size of a toy**, creating an immersive experience inside Andy's backyard. Surrounded by **oversized toys, building blocks, and Christmas lights**, this area is perfect for **families and Pixar fans**.

RC Racer – A High-Speed Halfpipe Ride

Ride Type: Thrill ride, halfpipe coaster
Height Requirement: 1.20m (3'11")

Duration: 1 minute
Thrill Level: (Moderate-High)

Inspired by RC, the remote-controlled car from **Toy Story**, this ride **swings riders back and forth on a U-shaped track**, similar to a skateboard halfpipe. It's one of the **most intense rides in the land**.

Ride Experience:

Strap in and speed **back and forth at increasing heights**

Feel the **weightlessness at the highest point** before plunging back down

Short but **high-adrenaline** experience

Tip: Best for **thrill-seekers**. Try to ride early in the day to **avoid long queues**.

Toy Soldiers Parachute Drop – A Drop Tower for the Whole Family

Ride Type: Family-friendly drop tower
Height Requirement: 0.81m (2'8")
Duration: 2 minutes
Thrill Level: (Moderate)

This **drop tower ride** is themed after **the Green Army Men from Toy Story**. Riders board **parachutes** and are lifted high before experiencing a **series of gentle drops**.

Ride Experience:

Enjoy a **bird's-eye view of the park** from the top

Feel a **series of small free-falls**, giving a fun **stomach-flipping sensation**

Perfect for **families and younger thrill-seekers**

Tip: Lines can get long, so ride **early in the morning** or use **Disney Premier Access**.

Slinky Dog Zigzag Spin – A Fun Coaster for Kids
Ride Type: Spinning coaster for young riders
Height Requirement: 0.81m (2'8")
Duration: 1 minute
Thrill Level: (Low)

This **gentle coaster** features **Slinky Dog looping in circles**, creating a **mild spinning effect** that's great for **younger children**.

Ride Experience:
Enjoy **light bouncing motions** as Slinky Dog moves along the track

A perfect **first coaster experience** for young visitors

Tip: Ideal for families with **small children** who want a **fun but mild** ride.

Ratatouille & Paris-Themed Attractions – A French Adventure

Location: Walt Disney Studios Park, La Place de Rémy

The **Parisian-themed area** of Walt Disney Studios Park transports visitors to a **storybook version of Paris**, inspired by **Pixar's Ratatouille**. With cobblestone streets, **quaint cafés, and intricate facades**, this area is one of the most **beautifully themed sections of the park**.

Ratatouille: The Adventure – A 4D Trackless Ride

Ride Type: 4D dark ride (trackless)
Height Requirement: No restrictions
Duration: 4 minutes
Thrill Level: (Mild)

Ratatouille: The Adventure is a **trackless dark ride that shrinks guests down to the size of Remy the rat** as they scurry through Gusteau's restaurant.

Ride Experience:

Board a **rat-shaped vehicle** and journey through **oversized kitchens, pantries, and dining rooms**

Experience **heat, wind, and water effects**

Escape **Chef Skinner** as he chases you through the restaurant

Tip: This ride is **very popular**. Use **Disney Premier Access** or ride **early in the day**.

Bistrot Chez Rémy – A Ratatouille-Themed Restaurant

Cuisine: French bistro
Price Range: €€€ (Moderate to Expensive)
Reservations: Recommended via **Disneyland Paris App**

This **immersive restaurant** makes you feel like you've **shrunk to Remy's size**, with oversized plates, forks, and bottle caps decorating the space.

Menu Highlights:

Ratatouille (of course!)

Filet de bœuf (beef fillet with sauce)

Traditional French desserts like crème brûlée

Tip: Make reservations early, as this is one of the **most popular restaurants** in Disneyland Paris.

Upcoming Attractions – What's Next for Walt Disney Studios Park?

Disneyland Paris is undergoing **major expansions** at Walt Disney Studios Park, including new lands based on **Frozen, Star Wars, and Marvel**.

Frozen-Themed Land – Kingdom of Arendelle (Opening 2025-2026)

One of the biggest expansions coming to Disneyland Paris is a **Frozen-themed land**, where guests can experience **the kingdom of Arendelle**, complete with:

A brand-new Frozen ride

A meet-and-greet area with Elsa and Anna

Themed dining and shopping experiences

Tip: Expect this to be **one of the most popular areas** once it opens!

Chapter 8

Rides & Attractions at Disneyland Paris

Disneyland Paris offers a mix of **thrill rides, family-friendly attractions, and immersive experiences** across **two parks: Disneyland Park and Walt Disney Studios Park**. Whether you're seeking **high-speed roller coasters, interactive adventures, or magical dark rides**, there's something for every visitor.

Must-Do Rides – The Unmissable Attractions

These are the **most popular, high-quality attractions** that define Disneyland Paris. Some are **exclusive to the park**, while others are **beloved Disney classics** with a Parisian twist.

1. Star Wars Hyperspace Mountain – A Thrilling Space Adventure

Location: Disneyland Park, Discoveryland
Height Requirement: 1.20m (3'11")
Thrill Level: (High)
Duration: 2 minutes

This **revamped version of Space Mountain** is one of the **most intense roller coasters in any Disney park**. Unlike its counterparts in the U.S., **Hyperspace Mountain features inversions, a launch, and high-**

speed turns inside a dark, outer-space setting with **Star Wars theming**.

What to Expect:
High-speed launch (0 to 44 mph in 2 seconds)

Three inversions (loop and corkscrews)

Immersive Star Wars battle scenes with Tie Fighters and X-Wings

Tip: Best for **thrill-seekers**. The queue can be long, so consider using **Disney Premier Access**.

2. Big Thunder Mountain – The Wildest Ride in the Wilderness

Location: Disneyland Park, Frontierland
Height Requirement: 1.02m (3'4")
Thrill Level: (Moderate)
Duration: 3 minutes

Considered **one of the best versions of Big Thunder Mountain worldwide**, this **mine train coaster** takes guests on a thrilling ride through the **rocky terrain of the Wild West**.

What to Expect:
Fast turns and sudden drops through dark tunnels

A breathtaking section under the Rivers of the Far West

Beautiful theming with waterfalls, caves, and cacti

Tip: This ride is **a fan favorite**, so expect **long waits during peak hours**. Ride **early in the morning** or use **Premier Access**.

3. Phantom Manor – A Dark & Eerie Haunted Mansion

Location: Disneyland Park, Frontierland
Height Requirement: No restrictions
Thrill Level: (Mild, spooky)
Duration: 7 minutes

Phantom Manor is **Disneyland Paris' unique take on the Haunted Mansion**, with a darker and **more cinematic storyline**. It follows the **mystery of the Ravenswood family**, a haunted bride, and a ghostly curse.

What to Expect:

Creepy animatronics and eerie storytelling

A haunting soundtrack unique to Disneyland Paris

A chilling Wild West ghost town finale

Tip: Great for **fans of eerie Disney attractions**. Not too scary for kids, but the **dark atmosphere** might be unsettling for young ones.

4. Pirates of the Caribbean – Set Sail for Adventure

Location: Disneyland Park, Adventureland
Height Requirement: No restrictions
Thrill Level: (Mild)
Duration: 7 minutes

This classic **boat ride** takes guests through **a swashbuckling pirate adventure.** The **Disneyland Paris version is one of the best**, with impressive sets and **Captain Jack Sparrow animatronics.**

What to Expect:

Waterfalls and small drops

Lifelike animatronic pirates in a burning village

Themed caves and a pirate skeleton lair

Tip: A great ride for **all ages. One of the best-themed attractions in the park.**

Family-Friendly Attractions

Disneyland Paris offers **a variety of attractions suitable for younger visitors and families**, focusing on **gentle rides, interactive experiences, and magical storytelling.**

1. It's a Small World – A Whimsical Boat Ride

Location: Disneyland Park, Fantasyland
Height Requirement: No restrictions
Thrill Level: (Low)
☐ **Duration:** 10 minutes

This **classic Disney boat ride** takes guests on a journey through **colorful animatronic scenes representing cultures around the world**.

What to Expect:

A cheerful, catchy song that plays throughout

Dancing dolls and vibrant costumes from different countries

A slow, gentle boat ride perfect for young children

Tip: A great attraction for relaxing and taking in the sights. **Wait times are usually moderate.**

2. Dumbo the Flying Elephant – A Classic Disney Ride

Location: Disneyland Park, Fantasyland
Height Requirement: No restrictions
Thrill Level: (Low)
Duration: 2 minutes

Dumbo is one of the **most iconic Disney rides**, allowing guests to **control their flying elephant** by **raising and lowering it in the air**.

What to Expect:

A gentle spinning ride

Colorful views of Fantasyland

Perfect for young kids

Tip: Ride early in the morning to **avoid long lines**.

3. Cars ROAD TRIP – A Scenic Pixar-Themed Journey

Location: Walt Disney Studios Park
Height Requirement: No restrictions
Thrill Level: (Low)
Duration: 10 minutes

This **tram-style ride** takes visitors on a **guided journey through Cars-themed landscapes**, featuring **animatronics, water effects, and interactive moments**.

What to Expect:

Scenes inspired by Pixar's Cars franchise

Special effects like explosions and water bursts

A relaxing, entertaining experience for all ages

Tip: Ideal for Pixar fans and families looking for a **mild ride**.

4. Mickey and the Magician – A Stunning Live Show

Location: Walt Disney Studios Park
Height Requirement: No restrictions
Thrill Level: (No thrill – live performance)
Duration: 30 minutes

This **Broadway-style show** follows **Mickey Mouse** as he learns the art of magic, with **appearances from classic Disney characters** like Elsa, Lumière, and Genie.

What to Expect:
Incredible stage effects and Disney music

A heartwarming storyline about dreams and magic

Perfect for all ages

Tip: Arrive **at least 15-20 minutes early** for a good seat.

Thrill Rides – High-Speed Adventures for Adrenaline Junkies

For visitors looking for **heart-pounding excitement**, Disneyland Paris features **some of the best thrill rides in the Disney Parks worldwide.** These attractions range from **high-speed roller coasters to immersive dark rides with intense effects**.

Hyperspace Mountain – A Star Wars-Themed Space Odyssey

Location: Discoveryland, Disneyland Park
Height Requirement: 1.20m (3'11")
Duration: 2 minutes
Thrill Level: (High)

Formerly known as Space Mountain, this **revamped version** takes guests on an intergalactic battle alongside the **Rebel Alliance**. Unlike its U.S. counterparts, Hyperspace Mountain in Disneyland Paris features:

A full 360-degree inversion (a rarity for a Disney coaster)

A high-speed launch from 0 to 44 mph (71 km/h) in seconds

A Star Wars-themed storyline with **TIE Fighters, X-Wings, and laser blasts**

Tip: Ride **at night** for an **even more immersive space battle experience**.

Pirates of the Caribbean – A Swashbuckling Adventure
Location: Adventureland, Disneyland Park
Height Requirement: None

Duration: 8 minutes
Thrill Level: (Mild-Moderate)

This **classic Disney dark ride** is **larger and more detailed than its American counterparts**. It features:

Two drops (one of which is in complete darkness!)

An elaborate pirate village with animatronic buccaneers

A storyline involving Captain Jack Sparrow

Tip: One of the best-themed rides in the park, especially **for fans of the films.**

Avengers Assemble: Flight Force – An Iron Man & Captain Marvel Coaster

Location: Avengers Campus, Walt Disney Studios Park
Height Requirement: 1.20m (3'11")
Duration: 1 minute 30 seconds
Thrill Level: (High)

This **high-speed indoor roller coaster** replaces Rock 'n' Roller Coaster and features:

A rapid launch from 0 to 57 mph (92 km/h) in **less than 3 seconds**

Multiple inversions and high-speed turns

Iron Man and Captain Marvel guiding you on a mission

Tip: One of the most intense rides in Disneyland Paris – great for Marvel fans and thrill-seekers.

The Twilight Zone Tower of Terror – A Drop into the Unknown

Location: Walt Disney Studios Park
Height Requirement: 1.02m (3'4")
Duration: 3 minutes
Thrill Level: (Moderate-High)

This **spine-chilling drop ride** takes guests into **The Twilight Zone**, featuring:

A randomized drop sequence, so no two rides are the same

Three unique storylines with different visual effects

A haunting, eerie atmosphere inside the abandoned Hollywood Tower Hotel

Tip: The **best view of Disneyland Paris** comes just before the drop – if you dare open your eyes!

Shows and Parades – The Heart of Disney Entertainment

Disneyland Paris is not just about rides—it offers **world-class shows, stage performances, and dazzling parades** that bring Disney stories to life.

Mickey and the Magician – A Must-See Live Show

Location: Walt Disney Studios Park, Animagique Theater
Duration: 30 minutes
Showtimes: Multiple daily performances
Experience Level: (Must-See)

This **award-winning stage show** follows Mickey Mouse as he learns magic from **Disney's greatest sorcerers**, featuring:

Live singing and dancing

Appearances by Genie, Elsa, Lumière, and Rafiki

Stunning special effects

Tip: Arrive early for the best seats—**this show is extremely popular**.

The Lion King: Rhythms of the Pride Lands – A Broadway-Caliber Spectacle

Location: Disneyland Park, Frontierland Theater
Duration: 30 minutes

Showtimes: Multiple daily performances
Experience Level: (Must-See)

This **stunning retelling of The Lion King** features:

Live African drumming and acrobatics

A reimagined take on classic songs like "Circle of Life"

Gorgeous costuming and puppetry

Tip: Check **show schedules in advance**, as times vary seasonally.

Disney Stars on Parade – A Daytime Spectacle

Location: Disneyland Park, Main Street, U.S.A.
Duration: 30 minutes
Showtime: Typically 5:30 PM (subject to change)
Experience Level: (Must-See)

This **vibrant parade** features:

Giant themed floats representing Disney movies

Characters like Mickey, Moana, and Frozen's Elsa & Anna

An energetic soundtrack and dancers

Tip: Find a spot near Sleeping Beauty Castle for the best views.

Disney Dreams! Nighttime Spectacular – The Grand Finale

Location: Disneyland Park, Sleeping Beauty Castle
Duration: 20 minutes
Showtime: Park closing time
Experience Level: (Must-See)

This **breathtaking nighttime show** features:

Dazzling fireworks over Sleeping Beauty Castle

Castle projections with scenes from Beauty and the Beast, Frozen, and The Lion King

A powerful musical score

Tip: Arrive 30-45 minutes early to secure a **good viewing spot** near the castle.

Chapter 9

Dining & Food at Disneyland Paris

Disneyland Paris offers a **wide variety of dining experiences**, ranging from **quick bites to gourmet meals**. Whether you're looking for a **fine-dining experience with Disney characters, themed restaurants, or budget-friendly meals**, the resort has

Best Restaurants in the Parks

Disneyland Paris has over **50 restaurants**, each with **unique themes, menus, and dining experiences**. From **table-service meals to quick bites, fine dining, and all-you-can-eat buffets**, the resort caters to all preferences.

Quick-Service Restaurants – Grab & Go Favorites

Quick-service restaurants offer **fast and affordable** meals without **reservations**. These spots are perfect if you want to maximize time on rides while still enjoying delicious food.

Café Hyperion (Discoveryland, Disneyland Park)
Location: Discoveryland
Price Range: €12 – €18 per meal
Cuisine: American fast food (burgers, fries, nuggets)

As the **largest quick-service restaurant in Disneyland Paris**, Café Hyperion is a great option for **a quick and filling meal**. It offers:

Classic cheeseburgers and crispy chicken nuggets

Vegan burger options

Plenty of seating inside the futuristic Star Wars-themed space

Tip: Since this is one of the busiest restaurants in the park, **avoid peak lunch hours (12-2 PM)** for faster service.

Fuente del Oro Restaurante (Adventureland, Disneyland Park)
Location: Near Big Thunder Mountain
Price Range: €14 – €20 per meal
Cuisine: Mexican

This **Tex-Mex-inspired eatery** is perfect for those craving **nachos, burritos, or churros**. It offers:

Delicious spicy beef and chicken fajitas

Refreshing frozen margaritas

Themed seating with a Wild West-Mexican ambiance

Tip: A great option if you're riding **Big Thunder Mountain**, as it's located right next to the attraction.

Table-Service Restaurants – A Sit-Down Experience

Table-service restaurants **require reservations** and offer a **more relaxed dining experience** with waiter service.

Captain Jack's – Restaurant des Pirates (Adventureland, Disneyland Park)

Location: Inside the Pirates of the Caribbean ride
Price Range: €35 – €50 per person
Cuisine: Caribbean-inspired seafood & Creole dishes

This **immersive, dimly lit restaurant** is located **inside the Pirates of the Caribbean attraction**, offering **waterfront views of the ride**. It serves:

Coconut shrimp, Creole chicken, and swordfish steak

A variety of rum-based cocktails

Tropical, pirate-themed décor

Tip: Book a table near the **waterfront** for the best ambiance.

Bistrot Chez Rémy (Walt Disney Studios Park)

Location: Ratatouille area
Price Range: €40 – €55 per person
Cuisine: French

Inspired by Disney's *Ratatouille*, this **Parisian-style bistro is shrunk down to rat-size proportions**, with oversized furniture and decorations. The menu includes:

Traditional French cuisine like ratatouille, steak, and gourmet desserts

A fine selection of wines

A beautifully themed interior straight out of the movie

Tip: One of the most popular restaurants at Disneyland Paris—reservations are a must!

Character Dining Experiences – Meet Disney Characters While You Eat!

Character dining is one of the **best ways to meet Disney characters** while enjoying **great food**. These restaurants allow you to take **photos and interact** with characters **without waiting in long lines**.

Auberge de Cendrillon (Cinderella's Inn) – Princess Dining

Location: Fantasyland, Disneyland Park
Price Range: €75 – €95 per person
Cuisine: French gourmet dining
Characters: Cinderella, Belle, Snow White, Ariel, Aurora

This **elegant, castle-style restaurant** is the **ultimate experience for Disney princess fans.** It offers:

A royal three-course meal with gourmet dishes

One-on-one time with Disney princesses at your table

A magical medieval-style dining hall

Tip: This is one of the **most expensive dining experiences** in Disneyland Paris, but it's worth it if you or your child **love Disney princesses.**

Plaza Gardens Restaurant – Breakfast with Mickey & Friends
Location: Main Street, U.S.A., Disneyland Park
Price Range: €45 – €55 per person
Cuisine: Buffet-style breakfast
Characters: Mickey, Minnie, Donald, Goofy

If you want to **start your morning with Mickey and friends**, this is the best place! It offers:

An all-you-can-eat breakfast buffet

Classic breakfast options (eggs, bacon, pancakes, fresh fruit)

Personal meet-and-greet time with Disney characters

Tip: Book in advance as **this is the only place in Disneyland Paris offering a character breakfast**.

The Lucky Nugget Saloon – Meet Toy Story & Western Characters

Location: Frontierland, Disneyland Park
Price Range: €20 – €35 per person
Cuisine: American BBQ
Characters: Woody, Jessie, and sometimes Mickey in cowboy gear

This **Western-themed restaurant** is perfect for those who love **Toy Story and cowboy-style BBQ food**. It features:

Ribs, BBQ chicken, and burgers

Live country music performances

A classic saloon-style setting

Tip: A good mid-range option for families who want a fun experience without the high price tag of princess dining.

Budget-Friendly Eats – Where to Eat on a Budget at Disneyland Paris

Dining at Disneyland Paris can be **expensive**, but there are several ways to **save money without sacrificing**

quality or experience. Many quick-service restaurants and snack stands offer **affordable yet filling meals**, while some locations provide **generous portions that can be shared**.

Tips for Saving Money on Food in Disneyland Paris

Bring Your Own Snacks – While full meals from outside are not allowed, you can bring **snacks, bottled water, and small sandwiches** to save on in-park food costs.

Opt for Quick-Service Restaurants – They are much cheaper than table-service restaurants and still provide **delicious Disney-themed meals**.

Look for Meal Deals & Combo Menus – Many restaurants offer **set meals** that include a **main dish, side, and drink**, often for a lower price than ordering items separately.

Refillable Water Bottles – **Water fountains are available throughout the park**, so bring a refillable bottle to avoid buying expensive bottled water.

Share Meals – Some portions, especially at **buffet-style restaurants**, can be shared to reduce costs.

Eat Outside the Park – If you have time, dining options in **Disney Village** or nearby **Val d'Europe shopping center** offer much cheaper meals.

Top Budget-Friendly Restaurants in Disneyland Paris

Market House Deli (Main Street, U.S.A.)

Location: Disneyland Park, Main Street, U.S.A.
Price Range: €7 – €12 per meal
Best for: Quick sandwiches, wraps, and light meals

This cozy deli offers **fresh sandwiches, baguettes, and wraps**, perfect for a quick and budget-friendly meal. Some great options include:

Ham & Cheese Baguette (€7.50) – Classic French sandwich with fresh ingredients

Chicken Caesar Wrap (€8.50) – A filling and flavorful option

Vegetarian Caprese Baguette (€8.00) – Fresh mozzarella, tomato, and pesto

Tip: Grab your food and enjoy a **picnic-style meal** in one of the park's open seating areas.

Casey's Corner (Main Street, U.S.A.)

Location: Disneyland Park, Main Street, U.S.A.
Price Range: €9 – €14 per meal
Best for: American-style hot dogs and fries

A classic Disney dining spot serving **generously sized hot dogs with various toppings**. Great budget-friendly choices include:

Classic Hot Dog & Fries (€10.50) – A simple yet filling meal

Chili Cheese Hot Dog & Fries (€12.50) – A flavorful upgrade with melted cheese and chili

Vegan Hot Dog (€9.50) – Plant-based option

Tip: Meal deals here offer **a drink, fries, and a hot dog** for a better price than buying them separately.

Fuente del Oro Restaurante (Frontierland)

Location: Disneyland Park, Frontierland
Price Range: €10 – €15 per meal
Best for: Tex-Mex lovers on a budget

A great place for **flavorful Mexican-inspired dishes** with **large portions at reasonable prices**. Popular items include:

Beef Burrito & Side Salad (€12.99) – A well-portioned, hearty meal

Chicken Fajitas (€13.50) – Served with grilled veggies and tortilla wraps

Churros with Chocolate Sauce (€5.50) – A budget-friendly dessert option

Tip: The portions are quite large—consider sharing a meal!

Hakuna Matata Restaurant (Adventureland)

Location: Disneyland Park, Adventureland
Price Range: €12 – €16 per meal
Best for: African-inspired dishes and chicken-based meals

One of Disneyland Paris's **most unique counter-service restaurants**, offering flavorful, filling meals:

Chicken Strips with Rice & Sauce (€13.99) – A great balance of protein and carbs

Vegetable Curry with Rice (€12.99) – A delicious plant-based option

Hakuna Fries (Spicy Potato Wedges) (€4.99) – A great budget-friendly snack

Tip: The rice-based dishes are filling and good for sharing.

Pizzeria Bella Notte (Fantasyland)

Location: Disneyland Park, Fantasyland
Price Range: €10 – €14 per meal
Best for: Affordable Italian food

A **Lady and the Tramp-themed pizzeria** serving simple yet delicious Italian dishes:

Margarita Pizza (€10.99) – Classic, affordable, and shareable

Pasta with Tomato Sauce & Parmesan (€12.50) – A hearty, budget-friendly meal

Tiramisu (€5.99) – A small but tasty dessert

Tip: Pizza portions are big enough to share—a great way to save money!

Cowboy Cookout Barbecue (Frontierland)

Location: Disneyland Park, Frontierland
Price Range: €13 – €17 per meal
Best for: BBQ lovers on a budget

Serving **grilled meats, BBQ ribs, and classic comfort food**, this is one of the **best value-for-money** restaurants in the park. Some top choices include:

BBQ Chicken & Fries (€14.99) – A hearty, filling meal

Pork Ribs & Coleslaw (€16.50) – Great for meat lovers

Vegetarian BBQ Burger (€13.99) – A plant-based option

Tip: This restaurant often has live country music performances, making it a fun experience!

Budget-Friendly Snacks & Quick Bites

For visitors who don't want to spend much on full meals, there are **plenty of snack kiosks offering quick, budget-friendly food options**:

Mickey Pretzels (€4.50) – Found throughout the park

Popcorn (€5.00) – Available in both sweet and salted varieties

French Crepes (€4.99) – Freshly made and a delicious snack

Ice Cream Cones (€4.99) – Perfect for a quick refreshment

Croissants & Pastries (€3.99) – Found at Market House Deli and bakeries

Tip: If you're on a **tight budget**, sticking to **snack kiosks and quick bites** can help stretch your food budget while still enjoying delicious treats!

Chapter 10

Shopping & Merchandise at Disneyland Paris

Shopping is an **essential part of the Disneyland Paris experience**, offering everything from **exclusive Disney merchandise** to **personalized souvenirs** and limited-edition collectibles. Whether you're looking for **plush toys, apparel, home décor, themed accessories, or attraction-specific memorabilia,** the parks and Disney Village offer a **wide variety of shopping options.**

Best Shops for Souvenirs at Disneyland Paris

Disneyland Paris has **dozens of shops**, each offering something unique. Some focus on **classic Disney characters**, while others are themed around **specific attractions, movies, or experiences.** Here are the **must-visit shops** to find the best souvenirs.

Emporium (Main Street, U.S.A.) – The Largest Store in Disneyland Paris
Location: Disneyland Park, Main Street, U.S.A.
Best for: Classic Disney souvenirs, plush toys, apparel, homeware

Emporium is the **largest store in Disneyland Paris**, offering a **huge selection of merchandise**. This is the **go-to place** if you want to grab souvenirs without visiting multiple stores. You'll find:

Disney Character Plush Toys – Mickey, Minnie, Stitch, and more

Disney-themed Clothing – T-shirts, hoodies, pajamas, and accessories

Mugs, Home Décor & Kitchenware – Mickey-shaped mugs, plates, and decorations

Keychains, Stationery & Pins – Affordable keepsakes

Tip: This shop can get very crowded at park closing time—shop earlier in the day if possible!

World of Disney (Disney Village) – Best One-Stop Shopping Spot

Location: Disney Village (outside the parks, near the entrance)
Best for: A mix of everything—perfect for last-minute shopping

World of Disney is the **flagship store of Disneyland Paris** and **one of the biggest** Disney stores in Europe. If you don't want to shop inside the parks, this store offers **almost everything in one place**, including:

Paris-themed Disney Souvenirs – Mickey with the Eiffel Tower, Ratatouille-inspired items

Exclusive Disneyland Paris Apparel – Jackets, caps, and themed outfits

Jewelry & Watches – Featuring Disney princesses, Mickey & Friends designs

Limited-Edition Pins & Collectibles

Tip: You don't need a park ticket to shop here—great for last-minute gifts before leaving.

Thunder Mesa Mercantile Building (Frontierland) – Western & Cowboy-Themed Merchandise
Location: Disneyland Park, Frontierland
Best for: Western, cowboy, and Toy Story-themed souvenirs

This shop is **perfect for fans of Frontierland and cowboy aesthetics**. Here you can find:

Cowboy Hats & Bandanas – Dress up as a cowboy or cowgirl

Frontierland-Themed Apparel – Flannel shirts, rustic Disney merch

Woody & Jessie Toys (Toy Story) – Sheriff Woody dolls, Toy Story-themed clothing

Tip: If you love **Big Thunder Mountain** or Toy Story, this shop is a must-visit!

La Boutique du Château (Fantasyland) – Best for Princess & Fairytale Merchandise

Location: Disneyland Park, Fantasyland (inside Sleeping Beauty Castle)
Best for: Disney Princess costumes, fairy tale-themed gifts

A **dreamy store inside Sleeping Beauty Castle**, this boutique is **perfect for princess fans**. You'll find:

Princess Dresses & Costumes – Cinderella, Belle, Elsa, and more

Disney Princess Crowns & Wands – For kids and collectors

Jewelry & Accessories – Inspired by Disney fairytales

Tip: This is the best shop for high-quality Disney princess merchandise—ideal for gifts!

Star Traders (Discoveryland) – Best for Star Wars & Marvel Fans

Location: Disneyland Park, Discoveryland
Best for: Star Wars, Marvel, and sci-fi-themed souvenirs

If you're a **fan of Star Wars or Marvel**, this shop is **a must-visit**. It specializes in:

Star Wars Lightsabers – Build-your-own or pre-made options

Marvel Superhero Gear – Spider-Man, Avengers apparel & accessories

Star Wars Collectibles & Action Figures – Including exclusive Disneyland Paris editions

Tip: You can customize your own lightsaber here!

Exclusive Merchandise – What You Can ONLY Buy at Disneyland Paris

Certain items are **exclusive to Disneyland Paris**, meaning you **won't find them in any other Disney park**. These are **the best souvenirs** for collectors and Disney fans looking for something unique.

Disneyland Paris 30th Anniversary & Special Event Merchandise

Limited Edition Disneyland Paris 30th Anniversary Ears – Special design for the park's anniversary

Commemorative Pins & Keychains – Featuring Disneyland Paris-exclusive logos

Anniversary Spirit Jerseys – Cozy, collectible clothing with unique designs

Tip: These items **sell out fast**, so grab them early in your visit!

Ratatouille & Paris-Themed Souvenirs

Since Disneyland Paris is home to **Ratatouille: The Adventure**, there are exclusive Paris-inspired items, including:

Chef Remy Plush Toys – Only available in Disneyland Paris

Parisian-Style Disney Mugs & T-Shirts – Featuring the Eiffel Tower & Disney characters

Ratatouille Recipe Books & Kitchenware – Cook like Remy!

Tip: These souvenirs are mainly found at **Chez Marianne – Souvenirs de Paris** in Walt Disney Studios Park.

Phantom Manor & Adventureland Collectibles

Some of the **most unique Disneyland Paris-exclusive souvenirs** come from **Phantom Manor** (Frontierland) and Adventureland.

Phantom Manor Haunted House Figurines – Perfect for Disney collectors

Pirates of the Caribbean-Themed Accessories – Pirate hats, swords, and Jack Sparrow merchandise

Exclusive Disneyland Paris Ride Posters – Artistic prints of classic attractions

Tip: These are rare collectibles, so they make great unique gifts!

Limited-Edition Disneyland Paris Pins
Disneyland Paris releases **exclusive pins** throughout the year, many of which are:

Attraction-Specific – Featuring rides like Big Thunder Mountain & Phantom Manor

Seasonal (Christmas, Halloween, New Year's) – Special festive designs

Limited-Edition (LE) – Only available in small batches

Tip: Check out Pueblo Trading Post (Frontierland) for the best pin selection.

Disney Collectibles & Limited-Edition Items – A Magical Treasure Hunt
For serious **Disney fans, collectors, and enthusiasts**, Disneyland Paris offers a variety of **exclusive and limited-edition merchandise** that can only be purchased

inside the resort. These items are **often released in small quantities**, making them **highly sought-after and valuable**.

What Kind of Collectibles Can You Find?

Limited-Edition Pins – Collectible Disney trading pins featuring characters, attractions, and anniversary designs.
Exclusive Disneyland Paris Plush Toys – Special versions of Mickey, Minnie, and other Disney characters dressed in Paris-themed outfits.
Anniversary & Seasonal Merchandise – Unique items celebrating special milestones (e.g., Disneyland Paris' 30th Anniversary Collection).
Park-Exclusive Figurines & Statues – Limited-run sculptures of beloved Disney characters and rides.
Attraction-Themed Merchandise – Items inspired by iconic rides like **Phantom Manor, Pirates of the Caribbean, and Ratatouille**.
Limited-Edition Ears & Apparel – Special Mickey and Minnie ear headbands and clothing available only at Disneyland Paris.
Disney Artwork & Lithographs – Stunning, park-exclusive art pieces featuring classic and modern Disney designs.

Where to Find Exclusive Collectibles at Disneyland Paris?

The Storybook Store (Main Street, U.S.A.)

Location: Disneyland Park, Main Street, U.S.A.
Best for: Limited-edition books, artwork, and collectibles

This beautifully designed store specializes in **Disney books, artwork, lithographs, and collector's items**. It's a **must-visit for serious Disney fans** looking for **rare or high-end souvenirs**.

Tip: Keep an eye out for **signed artwork and limited-edition prints** featuring Disneyland Paris landmarks.

Harrington's Fine China & Porcelains (Main Street, U.S.A.)

Location: Disneyland Park, Main Street, U.S.A.
Best for: High-quality Disney figurines, sculptures, and home décor

One of the **classiest stores in the park**, Harrington's offers **beautiful porcelain figurines, hand-painted collectibles, and exclusive Disney sculptures**.

Tip: Some items here are **limited edition**, and once they're gone, they won't be restocked—so grab them while you can!

Thunder Mesa Mercantile (Frontierland)
Location: Disneyland Park, Frontierland
Best for: Western-themed and Phantom Manor collectibles

A great place for fans of **Phantom Manor and Big Thunder Mountain Railroad**, this store sells **themed merchandise, posters, and ride-exclusive souvenirs**.

Tip: Phantom Manor fans can find **exclusive artwork, books, and pins** celebrating the eerie attraction.

Star Traders (Discoveryland)
Location: Disneyland Park, Discoveryland
Best for: Star Wars collectibles and sci-fi merchandise

This is **the ultimate shopping spot for Star Wars fans**, featuring **exclusive Star Wars figurines, lightsabers, droids, and apparel**.

Tip: Some **customizable droids and lightsabers** are available, making them unique souvenirs.

Chez Marianne (Souvenirs de Paris) (Walt Disney Studios Park)
Location: Walt Disney Studios Park, near Ratatouille: The Adventure
Best for: Parisian-themed Disney souvenirs and Ratatouille merchandise

A **beautiful French-inspired store**, offering exclusive **Ratatouille-themed gifts, Parisian Disney souvenirs, and stylish home décor**.

Tip: Look for **limited-edition Ratatouille kitchenware**, including adorable chef's hats and aprons.

The Disney Gallery (Disney Village)
Location: Disney Village
Best for: High-end Disney artwork, sculptures, and limited-edition collectibles

This store is **outside the parks**, but it's a **treasure trove of unique Disney art, sculptures, and signed collectibles**.

Tip: If you're looking for **rare Disneyland Paris artwork**, this is the place to visit.

How to Find Limited-Edition Merchandise?
Check Disneyland Paris' Official Website & App – Special releases are often announced online.
Follow Disney Social Media & Fan Pages – Many Disney collectors post updates about new releases.
Ask Cast Members in Stores – They often know about upcoming limited-edition releases.
Look for Annual Passholder-Exclusive Items – Some collectibles are only available to Disneyland Paris Annual Passholders.

Final Thoughts

Shopping at Disneyland Paris is **more than just buying souvenirs**—it's about finding **exclusive Disney collectibles, rare merchandise, and limited-edition treasures** that make for **perfect mementos of your visit**. Whether you're a casual Disney fan or a serious collector, there's **something magical waiting to be discovered** in the shops of Disneyland Paris!

Pro Tip: If you see a limited-edition item you love, **buy it immediately**—Disneyland Paris collectibles sell out quickly and are rarely restocked!

Chapter 11

Entertainment & Special Events at Disneyland Paris

Disneyland Paris is not just about rides—it's a **world of entertainment, dazzling performances, and seasonal celebrations** that bring Disney magic to life in unforgettable ways. From **spectacular fireworks and character meet-and-greets** to **seasonal events like Halloween and Christmas**, the park offers **year-round entertainment** that ensures every visit feels special.

Seasonal Events at Disneyland Paris

Disneyland Paris transforms throughout the year to celebrate special events with **decorations, themed shows, exclusive merchandise, and special character appearances**.

Disney Halloween Festival (October - Early November)

One of the most anticipated annual events, Disneyland Paris goes **full spooky mode** with:
Halloween decorations & themed parades – Pumpkins, ghosts, and Disney villains take over Main Street, U.S.A.
Mickey's Halloween Celebration Parade – A lively procession featuring Disney characters in Halloween

costumes.
Disney Villains Meet & Greets – Maleficent, Jafar, Ursula, and others make rare appearances.
Spooky snacks & treats – Halloween-themed food, like ghost-shaped pastries and pumpkin spice drinks.
Nighttime entertainment – The castle is lit with **spooky projections and eerie music**.

Tip: For the ultimate Halloween experience, visit during **Disney's Halloween Party (select nights in late October)**, where the park stays open late with **exclusive shows and a villain takeover!**

Disney Enchanted Christmas (Mid-November - Early January)

Disneyland Paris at Christmas is pure magic! With festive lights, holiday music, and snowfall on Main Street, U.S.A., this is one of the **best times to visit**.

What to Expect?
Mickey's Dazzling Christmas Parade – A heartwarming parade with Santa, Mickey, and friends in holiday outfits.
Sleeping Beauty Castle Illumination – A special Christmas light show with snowfall effects.
Meet Santa Claus & Disney Characters in Christmas Costumes – Perfect for holiday photos.
Festive Food & Drinks – Christmas cookies, hot chocolate, and themed holiday meals.

Christmas Markets in Disney Village – A charming market selling holiday gifts and treats.

Tip: Book early! Christmas is **one of the busiest times** at Disneyland Paris, and special holiday-themed dining experiences **sell out quickly**.

Other Seasonal Events

New Year's Eve Celebration (December 31st) – Special fireworks, a party atmosphere, and extended park hours.
Valentine's Day at Disneyland Paris (February 14th) – Romantic experiences, limited-edition treats, and couples' photo opportunities.
Disney's Easter Festival (March - April) – Easter egg hunts, themed snacks, and a springtime parade.
Spring & Summer Celebrations – Includes events like the **Disneyland Paris Pride Festival** and themed summer performances.

Fireworks & Nighttime Shows at Disneyland Paris

Disney Dreams! Nighttime Spectacular

Location: Sleeping Beauty Castle
Time: Typically at park closing

This **breathtaking show** features:

Fireworks, lasers, fountains, and music that bring classic Disney stories to life.

Projections on Sleeping Beauty Castle, transforming it into scenes from Disney movies.

Beloved songs from Disney films like *The Lion King, Beauty and the Beast, and Frozen.*

Tip: Arrive **at least 45 minutes early** to secure a good viewing spot near the castle.

Other Evening Shows
The Lion King: Rhythms of the Pride Lands – A Broadway-style live musical with acrobatics and drumming.
Disney Illuminations – A stunning mix of projections, fireworks, and music.
Dance Parties & Seasonal Night Shows – Special nighttime entertainment during events like **Disney Halloween Party** or **New Year's Eve**.

Character Meet & Greets – Where to Find Your Favorite Disney Characters

One of the **highlights of Disneyland Paris** is the chance to meet **beloved Disney characters** for photos, autographs, and special moments.

Meet Classic Disney Characters
Main Locations:

Main Street, U.S.A. – Mickey, Minnie, and classic Disney friends.

Fantasyland (Princess Pavilion) – Meet Disney Princesses like Cinderella, Belle, and Aurora.

Adventureland – Jack Sparrow, Aladdin, and Jasmine.

Tip: Character schedules change daily, so check the **Disneyland Paris app** for real-time updates.

Meet Pixar & Marvel Heroes
Walt Disney Studios Park is the best place for Pixar and Marvel character encounters!

Toy Story Playland – Buzz Lightyear and Woody.

Marvel Avengers Campus – Spider-Man, Iron Man, and Captain America.

Ratatouille Attraction Area – Remy and Emile from *Ratatouille*.

Tip: Avengers Campus has **interactive meet-and-greets** where superheroes might **train new recruits**—so get ready!

Meet Disney Villains (Seasonal)

Disney Villains are usually only available during Halloween and special events.

Best locations to find villains:

Maleficent & Jafar – **Adventureland**

The Evil Queen & Ursula – **Fantasyland**

Darth Vader & Star Wars characters – **Discoveryland (Starport)**

Tip: The best time to meet villains is during **Mickey's Halloween Party**, when they appear in special areas.

Final Thoughts – A Non-Stop Disney Spectacle!

Disneyland Paris **never stops entertaining**. Whether you visit during **Halloween, Christmas, or any season**, there's always something special happening. With **fireworks lighting up the night sky, characters greeting guests, and seasonal celebrations transforming the parks**, Disneyland Paris is a **magical experience year-round**.

Pro Tip: Use the **Disneyland Paris app** to check daily showtimes and **character locations** so you don't miss out on your favorite events!

Chapter 12

Tips & Tricks for a Smooth Visit to Disneyland Paris

A trip to Disneyland Paris is an unforgettable experience, but **crowds, long wait times, and planning mishaps** can make it less enjoyable if you're not prepared. To **maximize your time and enjoy every moment**, it's important to know how to **avoid long queues, optimize your visit, and make the most of the park's services**.

Best Ways to Avoid Long Queues at Disneyland Paris

Waiting in long lines can take up a huge portion of your day, but **smart planning and a few tricks** can help you **spend more time enjoying the attractions rather than waiting in line**.

Visit During Off-Peak Times

The best way to **avoid crowds** is to **choose the right time to visit**.

Best Months for Fewer Crowds: Mid-January to Mid-March – After the holiday season, crowds are significantly lower.

Mid-September to Early November – School is in session, so fewer visitors.
Weekdays (Tuesday – Thursday) – Avoid weekends when locals visit.

Avoid High-Crowd Periods:
School holidays in France & Europe (April, July-August, and December).
Public holidays & long weekends – French and UK holidays increase visitor numbers.
Special event days – During **Halloween and Christmas**, the parks are extremely crowded.

Tip: Check **French school vacation schedules** before booking your trip.

Arrive Early – "Rope Drop" Strategy

Arriving before the park opens (a strategy called "Rope Drop") gives you a huge advantage!

Gates open **30–45 minutes before official opening time**, so get there early.

Prioritize the most popular attractions **right after the park opens**, when wait times are shortest.

Go directly to major rides like Big Thunder Mountain, Peter Pan's Flight, or Avengers Assemble: Flight Force to ride with minimal waiting.

Tip: If you're staying at a **Disney Hotel**, you get access to **Extra Magic Time**, which allows you to enter the park **up to an hour early!**

Use Disney Premier Access (Skip-the-Line Service)

If you want to skip queues **entirely**, consider purchasing **Disney Premier Access.**

Disney Premier Access Ultimate: Allows you to skip the queue **once per ride** for most major attractions.

Disney Premier Access One: Lets you skip the queue for **a single ride** (useful for high-demand attractions).

Tip: Premier Access is available **via the Disneyland Paris app**. Book early as slots sell out quickly!

Prioritize Single Rider Lines

Some attractions offer **Single Rider queues**, which move **much faster** than regular lines.

Best rides for Single Rider queue:

RC Racer (Walt Disney Studios Park)

Ratatouille: The Adventure

Hyperspace Mountain

Avengers Assemble: Flight Force

Tip: Single Rider queues are perfect if you **don't mind riding alone**—your group will be split up.

Ride During Parades & Shows

While many visitors watch **parades and shows**, attraction wait times **drop significantly**.

Best time to ride with shorter queues:

During Disney Stars on Parade (usually mid-afternoon).

During nighttime fireworks shows – Some rides stay open during the fireworks, and queues are much shorter.

Tip: If you've already seen the parade before, **use this time to ride popular attractions with shorter waits!**

Eat at Off-Peak Hours to Save Time

Food lines can be long, especially around **12:00 PM – 2:00 PM** and **6:00 PM – 8:00 PM**.

Best strategy:

Have an **early or late lunch** (before 11:30 AM or after 2:30 PM).

Have **dinner before 6:00 PM** to avoid long lines.

Tip: Many restaurants accept **mobile orders via the Disneyland Paris app**, so you can skip the lines!

Use the Disneyland Paris App for Live Updates

The **Disneyland Paris app** is **essential** for skipping long lines!

Check **real-time wait times** for all attractions.

Use **the interactive map** to navigate the parks efficiently.

Book **Disney Premier Access** directly in the app.

Tip: Turn on **notifications** so you get **live updates on ride closures and queue times**!

Take Advantage of Ride Reopening After Temporary Closures

If a ride **temporarily closes due to weather or technical issues**, many people leave the queue. **Once it reopens, wait times are often much shorter!**

How to use this trick?

Stay nearby if a popular ride is closed temporarily.

Refresh the Disneyland Paris app to check when the ride reopens.

Be ready to queue immediately when it does—most guests won't realize it's back open yet!

Tip: This strategy works especially well for **Big Thunder Mountain, Indiana Jones, and Crush's Coaster**.

Visit Walt Disney Studios Park First (If You Want to Ride Crush's Coaster)

Crush's Coaster (one of the most popular rides) has **no Premier Access option**, so queues are always long.

Best Strategy:

Arrive early and go straight to Crush's Coaster (before it reaches 60+ minute wait times).

Then move to Ratatouille or Avengers Campus before those lines get too long.

Tip: Crush's Coaster has a Single Rider queue—use it if you don't mind riding alone!

Use Hotel Early Entry (Extra Magic Time)

If you stay at a Disney Hotel, you can enter the park up to 1 hour early!

Best rides to do during Extra Magic Time:

Big Thunder Mountain

Peter Pan's Flight

Hyperspace Mountain

Ratatouille: The Adventure

Tip: If you're staying off-site, consider booking a **breakfast reservation at a Disney hotel** to enter the park earlier.

Mobile Apps & Tech Tips – The Smart Way to Navigate Disneyland Paris

Disneyland Paris has embraced technology to **make visiting easier**. Whether it's checking ride wait times, booking restaurants, or using digital tickets, your phone can be your **best tool** during your trip.

Download the Disneyland Paris App (A Must-Have!)

The **official Disneyland Paris app** is **essential** for a smooth visit. It allows you to:
Check real-time wait times for rides
View show schedules & character meet-and-greet locations
Use the interactive park map to find attractions, restaurants, and facilities
Book restaurants & manage reservations
Access Disney Premier Access (skip-the-line service)
Purchase tickets & manage your booking

Pro Tip: Download the app **before** you arrive and set up your account in advance.

Where to Download:
iOS (Apple App Store)

Android (Google Play Store)

Get Disney Premier Access (Skip-the-Line Service)
Disney Premier Access (DPA) is **a paid service** that lets you skip the regular queues on certain attractions. There are two options:

Disney Premier Access One – Pay per ride to skip the queue.

Disney Premier Access Ultimate – Pay a higher price for unlimited priority access to participating attractions.

Tip: Popular rides like Avengers Assemble: Flight Force and Big Thunder Mountain often have long lines, so Premier Access can save **hours** of waiting.

Free Disneyland Paris Wi-Fi – Stay Connected!
Wi-Fi is available throughout Disneyland Paris, including:

Disneyland Park

Walt Disney Studios Park

Disney Village

Disney Hotels

Tip: The network is free, but it can slow down in crowded areas. If you need stable internet, consider using a **local SIM card** or an **eSIM** (for international visitors).

Mobile Payment & Digital Tickets
Disneyland Paris now supports Apple Pay, Google Pay, and contactless credit card payments.

Use digital tickets on your phone instead of printing them—this saves time at the entrance.

Magic Pass (for hotel guests) – This **all-in-one card** acts as your hotel room key, park ticket, and meal voucher.

Accessibility & Disability Services at Disneyland Paris
Disneyland Paris is committed to making the park **inclusive** and accessible for guests with disabilities, mobility issues, and special needs. The park offers **priority access services, adapted facilities, and dedicated support** for those who need assistance.

Priority Access & Easy Access Cards

Guests with disabilities or special needs can apply for:

Priority Access Card – Provides **skip-the-line access** to attractions, shows, and character meet-and-greets.

Easy Access Card – Allows access to dedicated attraction entrances but does not provide immediate entry.

How to Apply:

Visit City Hall (Disneyland Park) or Studio Services (Walt Disney Studios Park) with **medical proof** (e.g., disability card, doctor's certificate).

Cards are **valid for the entire duration of your stay**.

Tip: Bring all necessary documents **in advance** to avoid delays.

Wheelchair & Mobility Services

Wheelchair Rentals: Available at both parks for a **refundable deposit of €50**.

Attraction Accessibility: Some rides have **adapted boarding procedures** for wheelchair users.

Elevators & Ramps: Available in many areas, including Disney Village.

Tip: Not all rides allow wheelchair access, so check with **Cast Members** before queuing.

Visual & Hearing Impairment Assistance

For Visually Impaired Guests:

Braille park maps are available at Guest Services.

Certain attractions offer **audio descriptions**.

For Hearing-Impaired Guests:

Some shows have **sign language interpretation** (check schedules in advance).

Induction loops are available for guests with hearing aids.

Contact Information:

Guest Relations: +33 1 60 30 60 53

Email: dlp.communication.visiteurs@disney.com

Tip: If you need assistance, **notify Disneyland Paris in advance** to arrange special accommodations.

Dietary & Allergy-Friendly Dining Options

Disneyland Paris offers **allergy-friendly meals** for guests with dietary restrictions.

Request **special menus** at table-service restaurants.

Certain quick-service restaurants offer **gluten-free & vegetarian options**.

Guests with severe allergies can bring their **own food** with medical documentation.

Tip: Inform restaurant staff about **food allergies** when booking a table.

Bonus Tips for a Smooth Visit

Arrive Early – The best way to experience Disneyland Paris **without long waits** is to arrive **before the park opens**.

Use Single Rider Queues – If you don't mind riding alone, **single-rider lines** are much faster.

Bring a Power Bank – You'll use your phone a lot (for maps, reservations, photos), so keep a charger handy.

Dress Comfortably – Wear **good walking shoes**; you'll be on your feet for hours.

Pack for the Weather – Paris can be unpredictable—bring a **raincoat in winter** and **sunscreen in summer**.

Book Popular Restaurants in Advance – Dining spots like **Bistrot Chez Rémy and Captain Jack's** fill up quickly!

Final Thoughts – Be Smart & Enjoy the Magic!

A little planning goes a long way in making your Disneyland Paris visit **smooth, stress-free, and magical**. By using **technology, accessibility services, and smart tips**, you can **maximize your time, avoid common hassles, and focus on the fun.**

Pro Tip: Download the **Disneyland Paris app, arrive early**, and **use Priority Access if needed**—this will save you hours in queues!

Conclusion

Final Thoughts & Recommendations

A visit to **Disneyland Paris** is not just about exploring a theme park—it's about **stepping into a world of imagination, nostalgia, and unforgettable adventure**. Whether you're visiting for a single day or spending an entire week soaking in the magic, your experience will depend on **how well you plan, what you prioritize, and how you make the most of your time**.

This final section provides a **detailed summary of everything you need to know**, key takeaways, and expert recommendations to ensure your Disneyland Paris trip is nothing short of **extraordinary**.

Key Takeaways for a Smooth & Magical Visit
Plan Ahead for the Best Experience

Disneyland Paris is **a world-class destination**, and to get the most out of it, planning is essential. Here's how to ensure a **stress-free and smooth trip**:

Book your tickets in advance to secure the best prices and avoid long queues at the entrance.

Check the official Disneyland Paris app for real-time ride wait times, show schedules, and mobile food ordering.

Create a flexible itinerary that prioritizes your must-do attractions, shows, and dining experiences.

Pro Tip: The park is **less crowded on weekdays**, especially **Tuesdays through Thursdays**. If possible, avoid weekends and French school holidays.

Prioritize Attractions Based on Your Preferences

With **two parks, dozens of rides, live shows, character meet-and-greets, and special events**, it's **impossible** to do everything in one day. Instead, focus on **what matters most to you**.

Here's a breakdown of must-do attractions based on visitor preferences:

For Thrill Seekers

Star Wars Hyperspace Mountain (High-speed roller coaster)

Avengers Assemble: Flight Force (Marvel-themed roller coaster)

The Twilight Zone Tower of Terror (Free-fall drop ride)

Indiana Jones and the Temple of Peril (Outdoor looping coaster)

For Families & Kids

Peter Pan's Flight (Magical ride over Neverland)

Ratatouille: The Adventure (4D motion-based dark ride)

It's a Small World (Iconic family-friendly boat ride)

Buzz Lightyear Laser Blast (Interactive space shooter ride)

For Classic Disney Lovers

Character Meet-and-Greets (Check the app for schedules)

The Disney Stars on Parade (Daily afternoon parade)

Disney Dreams! Nighttime Spectacular (Fireworks & projections)

Pro Tip: If your trip is short, **Disney Premier Access** (paid fast-track service) can save you **hours of waiting** in line.

Budgeting Smartly & Finding the Best Deals

Disneyland Paris can be an **affordable trip or a luxury experience**, depending on **how you plan**. Here's how to make your trip cost-effective while still enjoying all the magic:

Money-Saving Strategies

Book Tickets in Advance – Prices vary depending on demand. Purchasing early usually guarantees lower rates.

Look for Hotel & Ticket Bundles – Staying at **a Disney hotel** often includes **park tickets and early entry** benefits.

Use Free Water Stations – Instead of buying bottled water, refill at hydration stations throughout the park.

Pack Your Own Snacks – Bringing small snacks can cut down food costs.

Annual Pass – Is It Worth It?

If you plan to visit **multiple times in a year**, an **Annual Pass** can **save you money** on **tickets, dining, and merchandise**. Some passes even offer **free parking and discounts on hotels**.

Pro Tip: Travel **during off-peak months** (January-March, September-November) for **cheaper tickets, fewer crowds, and shorter wait times**.

Making the Most of Entertainment & Special Events

Disneyland Paris is **more than just rides**. The park is **known for its world-class entertainment, seasonal events, and breathtaking nighttime spectaculars**.

Must-See Shows & Events

Disney Stars on Parade (Daily, featuring Mickey, Disney princesses, and Pixar characters)

Mickey and the Magician (Award-winning stage show with illusions and musical performances)

Disney Dreams! Nighttime Spectacular (Fireworks, lights, and projections on Sleeping Beauty Castle)

Seasonal Events to Watch For

Halloween Festival (October) – Special spooky decorations, villain meet-and-greets, and nighttime parties.

Disney Enchanted Christmas (November – January) – Christmas trees, snowfall on Main Street, and a festive parade.

Pride at Disneyland Paris (June) – A special **LGBTQ+ pride celebration** with exclusive entertainment.

Pro Tip: Special events **may require extra tickets**—check the official website **before** planning your visit.

Final Verdict – Is Disneyland Paris Worth It?

Absolutely! Whether you're a **Disney fan, a thrill seeker, or traveling with family**, Disneyland Paris is **a must-visit destination**. The mix of **classic Disney storytelling, thrilling attractions, and European charm** makes it **one of the best theme parks in the world**.

Final Pro Tip: Plan wisely, use the **Disneyland Paris app**, book **Disney Premier Access for top rides**, and arrive early to make the most of your trip.

Final Verdict: Disneyland Paris is 100% worth visiting—just be prepared, plan ahead, and enjoy the magic!

Printed in Great Britain
by Amazon